Resilient Now

A personal story

Dom Wharram

Publisher:

dCoached LLC
Publishing arm
909 County Road 19
Independence, MN. 55359

Copyright © 2025 by Dominic Wharram

All rights reserved. No part of this book may be reproduced or transmitted in any form or by any means, electronic or mechanical, including photocopy, recording, or by any information storage and retrieval system, except for brief quotations in critical reviews or articles, without the written permission of the publisher, except where permitted by law. For information address: dCoached LLC, Independence, MN.
www.dCoached.com

ISBN: 978-1-886084-11-7 (paperback)

ISBN: 978-1-886084-12-4 (eBook)

Internet addresses, phone numbers, and descriptions for access to professional services or any other organization printed in this book are offered as a potential resource and are not intended to imply endorsement or advice by the publisher or author. Further, the publisher and the author cannot vouch for the accuracy of such information since they are all outside our control.

Dedicated to:

<u>My family.</u> I am blessed by how many people consider me part of their family. And I delight in knowing the people I love and call my family.

<u>Linda.</u> It's no secret who you are to me.

<u>All the teachers in my life.</u> You are the angels that have surrounded me.

ACKNOWLEDGMENTS

Several People have provided professional insights and guidance during the writing of this book:

My wife, Linda and our Children – The first editors & the best.
Ang – My challenger. And I'm grateful!
Jenny – So much inspirational awesome in you. So much.
David – Thank you, for so much more than just guidance.
Matthew – Compassion and brilliance. Thanks for both.
Jon – Intentions matter. We know this to be true.
John – Thank you my long, long-time friend.
Chris – Grateful for our friendship. It's a good place to be.
Lona – We're lucky to have you as a friend.
Kristi –Rockstar. Always have been. I'm certain you always will be.
Mel – Thank you for sharing your story with me too.
There are others … and each of you know who you are.
Thank you.

Table of Contents:

Let's begin here: *3*

My story: *7*

    Really Young 9

    Elementary School 35

    Junior High & High School 69

    Next 111

7 mindsets to be Resilient Now *115*

    Listen to everything 122

    Provide value 124

    See through it 128

    Say, 'Yes, and …' 133

    Take responsibility 138

    Change 145

    Keep moving 149

    Some final thoughts: 152

About: *156*

    About the book: 156

    About resilience: 159

    BONUS CONTENT 162

    Be Brave: Resources 168

    About the author: 169

Purpose

Inspiration. Not easy given the topics, but it is the purpose of this book.

It may prompt introspection at times, as any enjoyable conversation might.

This book is part memoir, part self-help, but all of it is from my heart.

I share some of my childhood experiences, hoping to connect with those living in or healing from hardship.

If someone you love is dealing with something now or has in their past, perhaps this book can be insightful.

My aim is to encourage empowerment.

Disclosures:

Descriptive violence, alcohol and drug abuse, child neglect, death, and suicide are all topics addressed in real-world personal scenarios. If these subjects are triggering for you, please consider whether to read this book thoughtfully and with awareness.

All the quotes are mine unless I point out who they came from. I wrote them down as they came to me over the years. And finally, even where I have changed their names, all the folks I talk about are real people in my life.

Let's begin here:

I knew about hitchhiking. I knew my brothers had hitchhiked from one place to another often enough. I thought I would give it a try. I started out in Denver, Colorado, with a destination of Grand Forks, North Dakota, mapped out on a bunch of paper maps I had collected.

It took me four and half days of hitchhiking and making up stories and trying to figure out how to eat. During my four plus day trek, I slept behind roadside rest buildings or gas stations where no one would see me. When the people who picked me up from the side of the road where I stood with my duffle bag and thumb out, I was all smiles. They asked all the questions you might expect: Is everything OK? Do you need any help? Where are you headed to? Are you alone?

I lied. I lied to every single person, and I told some whoppers.

For example, I told folks: "I'm just heading to the next town." (And I had maps all lined out, so I knew what the next town was.) … and then I would explain with another lie, "it's a big challenge. My brother and I are racing each other. He started in the next town and is hitchhiking back to this town. I'm hitchhiking from this town to the next one. We have to call each other on these payphones to see who wins…" I had a fake phone number on a sheet of paper and when I told this lie, I would show them the piece of paper to really sell 'the big challenge'. I would just name the right cities, and I would smile with real excitement to encourage them to hurry so I would win the race. Since this was my go-to lie, I had to stop at just about every town along the way.

I share the whole story later in this book, but my last ride was from just north of Fargo to Grand Forks. I had the destination circled on my map; a specific house in mind, and I finally got there.

Once I was at that door, everything else in my head went blank. I couldn't see anything other than the doorway. It was like the whole world turned to thin air, and all that was left was a single screen door in front of a wooden door with a doorbell just to the side. I pushed the button, and everything else faded away.

The year was 1981. That was the summer between 7th and 8th grade for me. I was twelve years old. Everything I owned was in my school gym duffle bag. As far as I knew, no one knew I was going to knock on this door.

That story I just told was a pivotal moment in my young life, over 43 years ago.

Since then, I have not become a famous person. And my story isn't about rags to riches or anything dreamy like that. I'm just like you—someone determined to beat the odds, to rise above, and who had to battle against hardship quite often early on in life, and I share much of it in this book with you, plus how that has followed me into adulthood.

If you are the one dealing with hardship right now, or healing from trauma in your life – this book is for you.

If someone you love is dealing with or healing from hardship or trauma, I hope this book offers some insight for you to walk with them to a better place.

As I share, and you read, you will remember or think about your own experiences. This book isn't about who had it worse or who has the deepest wounds or greatest triumphs. You and I can both find people worse off than us. And both of us know people complaining about their lives when they haven't had to deal with even half of what we have had to deal with in our lives. And both of us know the rich and famous that others compare themselves to. None of those things are important in this book. You and I are the important people in this book. **That's why I wrote it: You and I are sitting down for a conversation, and it's personal.**

I look forward to the conversation!
My best to you,
- Dom

Notes:

My story:

> **"Miracles ... If you expect miracles, treat people like Angels."**

Pre-k through high school…

Resilient Now

Really Young

We all know that the surface story rarely tells the true story. You know, the short, 30 second thing we say about ourselves, or hear from others, or make up in our own head when we see someone for the first time.

The surface story for who I was as a young person is short, maybe a little interesting – but forgettable. If I didn't want to talk too much about it, I would say something like:

I had a normal childhood through kindergarten. I was the youngest of five boys. We lived in Colorado. My dad was retired Airforce and mom stayed at home raising us. Oh – and I could read pretty well before I even started kindergarten, so that's kind of interesting.

There is always more to someone's story. Here's the rest of that story…

Pre-k

We have all played the game where someone asks us to recall our earliest memory. For me, it's pulling up in our blue station wagon to the house in the forest. Our dad wasn't in the military any longer, and I don't have any memories of him as a military guy. I was only two or three years old at that point, and I was the only one of us five boys born in a civilian hospital. My brothers were all born on an air force base, and as far as I can remember, they all had that military buzz cut, but I don't think I ever did. Mom stayed home to raise us boys while dad traveled for work. I'm not sure what he did after the military, but here we were on twenty acres in the middle of the forest in Colorado Springs, but I loved that forest. And we had chickens to tend.

Alone in the forest

On those twenty acres in the middle of the Black Forest, at four years old, my job was to collect the eggs every day from our chicken coup on the edge of the deep forest. I could spend hours doing this chore. We also had a dog named Tramp that would do my chores with me. Often, instead of collecting eggs, we would play in the forest—maybe nap. Maybe we would even sleep out there overnight... or maybe two nights in a row. I even collected things like rocks and interesting pine needles and moss on all our adventures. There was an old cabin in the forest where I would keep the stuff I collected. Sounds idyllic, doesn't it? Everything seemed normal to me. I didn't know any different.

The truth of the matter was that I would stay away from the house as long as I could. Playing in the forest and collecting eggs took longer and longer every day, mainly because I wanted to stay away from the house. There was a very big difference between what our HOUSE sounded like and what the forest sounded like to me. The sounds at home included breaking glass and thrown dishes from time to time. There was the sound of loud voices YELLING at other loud voices. The words they were yelling were not pleasant words. I would hear the words, 'YOU!' and 'THEM' quite often, screamed at someone else. Those were words I knew meant someone was to blame for something. I would hear names – and know who was being blamed. My brother's names were blamed often. My parents' names were blamed often. My name was blamed often. 'THIS HOUSE!' was blamed often. And it seemed the only way to blame someone, or something was by YELLING it and maybe THROWING something or SLAMMING a door.

Sometimes the CRYING was loud too. Sometimes the crying was mixed with YELLING about who was to BLAME. Sometimes I heard the BELT on one of my brothers and that was LOUD. Sometimes that was followed by CRYING. Sometimes to cover up how loud the yelling was, the STEREO would be turned up LOUD on top of it all.

SLAMMING doors were loud. That usually meant someone was coming, leaving or running someplace to avoid the violence of a voice, a fist or a belt. I usually heard the words, 'GET BACK HERE…' followed by other angry words if I heard a door SLAMMED.

AND THERE WAS A SECOND THING GOING ON IN MY HEAD. I didn't just hear how loud it all was. In my head, I saw colors and shapes. None of the colors and shapes that go with yelling, loud music, crashing dishes, and belt whaps is pleasant. The shapes are ragged and pointed sharply, like shards of glass or the edge of a saw. The colors are not clear colors, as if there isn't enough light to see what colors they really are—the colors don't have names that we learned by looking at crayons, and they slam in and out of the picture too fast, and sometimes in frightening ways. I've learned there is a clinical name for this—but to my little brain, when those were the sounds I could SEE, it meant it was time to get to the woods. Or stay in the woods if I could see the noise as Tramp and I walked back into the yard.

In the forest, the shapes and sounds that go with blowing wind or silence or birds or the rustling of pine needles under my feet or Tramp's paws are like colorful whisps of smoke that start gently, rise and swirl pleasantly upward slowly. As they rise and grow and become more beautiful, smaller ones begin below to follow them. Like seedlings starting to grow. The colors all have names we know, and some are favorites. They all work together when they mingle upward. None of them crash into each other violently or disappear in scary ways. They fade, and new whisps grow.

It got to where I could be gone a couple days, and no one would come looking for me. I could pack some crackers and hide the peanut butter and jelly jars along with a butter knife in the egg basket, and I was good to go.

Bullet hole

My brothers loved their fun out in the forest too.

Dad was gone a lot, traveling for work. Mom stayed home with all us boys, but honestly, I can't remember seeing her around all that much. But I'm sure she was there. When mom and dad were home together – it was loud in the house. When they weren't home – it was still loud, and maybe even more so with just my brothers. They would keep the eight-track player on full volume, break into the gun closet, and take out the bolt-action rifle. I remember that's the one they took most often because it got stuck once when they were trying to shoot it. They were pushing, pulling, smacking that bolt with their hands, and at one point, a rock. I was somewhere between four and five years old then, and my oldest brother was thirteen or fourteen. All my brothers were one year apart from each other, and I was apart from them by a 4-year gap. I was the baby.

The gun became unstuck right when I was in front of it, and the bullet went right through my windbreaker blowing in the wind as I wore it. The bullet missed me, thankfully. My brothers made me hide that windbreaker and then later burn it in the firepit so mom and dad wouldn't know anything about how they would steal the guns. I suppose my parents would have been pretty mad that I had a bullet hole in my windbreaker. Good thing my brothers thought that through. It never dawned on me that I was almost shot or that if I had been shot, that it would have been a bad thing.

Forest Fire!

Even today, a forest is a real source of solace for me. Back when our family home was in the forest, I felt more at home out past the chicken coop with my crackers, peanut butter and jelly, and Tramp, than I did in our front yard. And I liked the chickens. I liked that I had a job. I liked that I had a purpose. Having a purpose is important, and I think I realized that at a very young age. The idea fed something in me that made it a very strong part of who I am today. In fact, as I look back – the idea of providing value (something I talk more about in the back of the book where I share what I've learned as part of the stories I share in this book) was born with my job of collecting eggs. I had a job; mom counted on me to bring in the eggs... and so, even if it took me a couple days, I would always go home with a basket full.

And there was Tramp. She was the first of the Angels in my life before a series of people over the years. We will get to them throughout the book, but about Tramp first:

She was my dog. She was an older dog, so she must have been part of our family way before I came along. But once I started collecting eggs, Tramp and I were never apart. My brothers had another dog, named Kimba. My mom and dad had a cat, Cookie-Jar, that I remember mom taking care of mostly. I still have a scar on my right hand where that cat bit me, so she and I never got along much. And Tramp had me.

How Tramp became my dog started with a neighbor kid who lived in a house somewhere else in the forest. He taught me to 'flick matches'. I thought it was pretty cool. Flicking a match is where you tear off a single match from a matchbook. Then you sort of hold the matchbook in such a way where you put the match between the striker and a finger on your other hand so you can 'swipe' the match as you slide your finger really fast forward, flicking it as it lights up. Don't try this at home – because when I did it by myself in the forest, I lit a patch of pine needles on fire by accident a few feet away.

Before I knew it, things were beyond what I could

manage as a 5-year-old. Tramp grabbed my shirt and pulled me away from the fire that I was trying to deal with, but I was getting closer to catching my clothes and hair on fire than putting it out. Once she and I were running away, she took off faster than me towards the house, letting folks back home know there was a problem.

I remember it all being dealt with before the forest burned down, but it was a pretty big fire, and we lost the old cabin as well as my collection of things.

I remember being hungry after the ordeal and going to bed having had only a piece of toast and a hard spanking on my rear. I don't remember much else, but I went to bed with visions of how Tramp grabbed my clothes and pulled me away from a growing flame that I couldn't handle. I will never forget that day.

From then on, she protected me like a mother. She probably did before that, but that's when I knew she and I were partners in this thing together. This 'thing' being that we lived in this house with plenty of noise, and we liked to go where there wasn't any.

Now, I'm not sure if she did things to get me to follow her out of the house or if she followed me—but I know we were together every time mom and dad were arguing or my brothers were fighting or up to something they shouldn't have been up to. We left the house, and we were just fine, even if it meant we were in the woods for a day or two.

I never told on my brothers for anything, not even the bullet hole, and I remember getting in trouble for 'losing' that windbreaker. I never tried to explain myself before a spanking, whether I deserved it or not. I just didn't talk. The first time I spoke out loud to someone was when I was about four or so, just a little before my first year in kindergarten. The cat was in trouble with porcupine needles, so my first words were 'kitty-cat' while I pointed to her under the couch where she was hiding, needing help. Dad handled it, I think. I never let anyone know she bit my hand when I tried to help her.

Some people have said I probably didn't talk because I had four brothers who probably did all the talking for me. It's been easy to let that be the answer people heard and assumed because that ended the conversation. The real story is that it seemed that mostly anytime someone talked in my home, it was to blame someone for something. And once blame was the topic, someone yelled louder than the first person. The yelling turned into things breaking because they were thrown, slammed, or someone was hit. And when things were thrown, slammed, or hit, all I could see was the noise. To me, talking never meant anything good was about to happen. So, I didn't talk. But when I saw the cat was hurt and the cat bit me for trying to help – I had to talk. So, I did. It was scary, but I did it, and I hid my bleeding hand in a pair of mittens so I couldn't be blamed for something that would start the yelling that followed blame in our home.

Bed without supper

I know 'going to bed without supper' doesn't sound like a big deal occasionally. But going to bed without supper was kind of normal in our home. Sometimes it was because I wasn't home to eat it if there was a meal on the table. I spent a lot of time in that forest, and no one seemed to ever come look for me when it would have been supper time. Other times when I was home, there just wasn't anyone around to make the food that should go on the table at supper time. I have more memories of making toast and eating peanut butter or whatever else might be around, out in the forest, than I do of family meals. If we did ever eat together, dad would have been home. At my father's table, there were three rules. He asked questions, and we answered. That was the only talking allowed. We ate with proper manners or were excused to stand behind our chair until we understood how to comply with proper manners. And we were to eat everything on our plate. No exceptions... or it would be saved for our next meal.

But after the forest fire, I was actually sent to my room without supper as punishment. At least I think it was supposed to be punishment by the sound of how I remember my mom's voice. That was OK, though. I headed to my room knowing I had crackers and peanut butter in the egg basket. Tramp came with me. We were fine.

Kindergarten

If I'm among friends talking about early school, I may joke and say something like, "yes … I flunked Kindergarten." It usually gets a good laugh and I don't really need to add much more. But the way it really worked is that my first year of kindergarten was split between two different schools. I started in Colorado Springs, where we had been living for a few years. My guess is that my brothers had all gone to this elementary school and now it was my turn. That school was just on the edge of the forest, and we must have all taken the bus to get there. What I do remember is that it was a small elementary school. I didn't attend it long enough to have made any friends that I remember, because our stay in the forest was coming to an end for some reason. Perhaps my Dad had a different job. I never asked, and so I don't know what made us move. But, midway through the year, we moved to Denver.

I remember that the elementary school there was much larger. But I behaved about the same in both schools. I liked the toys, especially the Lincoln logs and Legos. I also liked the crayons and blank paper. We didn't have any of these kinds of things at our house, so they all seemed new to me. We did have books in the house, and I had read all of them. Once we were all settled in Denver and I was going to school every day, the teacher learned I could read, she brought in some childhood books from something called the (SRA

Reading Laboratory) or 'SRA books' for me from some other classrooms. The SRA books were small little books that were mostly picture books with simple words. I was amused by them being so colorful with giant printing compared to chapter books I had already read, like The Hobbit, the Bible, The Red Badge of Courage, or all the books by C.S. Lewis. We also had a full Encyclopedia at home that I read from time to time, so, in comparison, the little SRA books were fun for me to just look at. They were very different than other things I had been reading.

But as far as memories go, I can't remember my teacher's name, the name of the school, whether my brothers went there too or not, or even how I got to and from school. I just remember the difference in those schools from the forest to the city, and it was much different. In the forest, there were just a few kids in the classroom, and the teacher brought out snacks for everyone. In the city, there were a lot more kids, it was louder, the rooms were bigger, and if you didn't bring snacks from home, there were no snacks. There was just the choice between snacks or quiet time. I had quiet time.

I remember my second year of kindergarten much better.

So – yes. I flunked kindergarten, but really – I think someone made a great choice to have me give it a second try.

Kindergarten - again

The only memories I have of my home life back then are the address of our house and that I was aware my brothers all smoked pot, did other drugs, and the police started showing up every once in a while.

Much later in life, as an adult, I drove by that childhood home one time to be sure it was a real place and not a story of a place – but a real place with a real memory. However, visiting that house seemed more like recalling a story compared to a real memory. I say that because I can tell you stories of what happened in that house, but mostly I have real memories of my school life more clearly. And really, just kindergarten.

Specifically, I remember my kindergarten teacher (second time around) very well. The first memory I have of him is that I was unable to explain to him who it was that taught me to read. As I think about it now, someone must have taught me, maybe a brother, but I have no memory of who or how, and no one has ever claimed teaching me. My mom was unaware that I could read when the teacher asked her. But I think she knew I could because I would read her Bible. At least I thought she knew that's what I was doing when I would take it from her bedside table. I would take her iconic green 'Living Bible' that every home must have had, I thought. But I remember her being very surprised about it talking to the teacher.

He had me show her that I could read by having me read a random page from The Hobbit. (If you haven't read this book, you need to go get it now and read it. It's a great book). He handed the paperback book to me, and as he did, he folded it open to a random page. I read it out loud and started to trail off in volume as I got into it, enjoying the story. He snapped me out of it, asking me who some characters were from other well-known books. After a few of those questions, my mom said to him, 'It is a mystery.' I do remember sitting there when she said those words and the teacher just smiling at me when she wasn't looking.

Later on in the year, I remember winning a science award. My teacher had entered me in an all-elementary school science program, and I built a model of the lunar lander on the moon in a diorama. None of my family ever knew I was even in the science program, much less that I got a blue ribbon for the work... as a kindergartener.

Looking back, he was the first Angel in my life, apart from my dog, Tramp. Mr. R was his name. He was my kindergarten teacher, and he knew I could read. This will sound strange, but he was the one who explained to me that what I was doing with books was called 'reading'.

He was the first person I know that caught on

about my home life. He seemed to understand that I didn't know how or didn't like doing all the things all the other kids were doing. So, he gave me a special project and a table in the classroom and didn't seem to care that all the other kids were doing different things than me during class. He handed me a model kit of the lunar lander, six colors of Testers paint bottles for models, a twelve pack of paint brushes, a stack of paper and cardboard, a shoebox full of sand, and a couple different bottles of glue. He also handed me two books checked out from the library in my name. He showed me they were checked out in my name and told me the date I needed to return them or check them out again. Later on, he introduced me to Mrs. K, the librarian who showed me all the books in the world! What a wonderful place Mrs. K owned (I thought).

Of the two books Mr. R handed me, one was about the lunar lander and was about an inch thick with pictures and lots of descriptions about the NASA project putting a person on the moon. The other smaller book had a blue cover, and it was full of knock-knock jokes. He asked me to show him what I could do with all that stuff he gave me. And he said the little blue book was to give me a smile every once in a while when I needed a break. He said I could tell him a joke anytime I wanted. I think he wanted me to start talking a little more now that I look back at that memory. It must have worked because I also remember him being surprised that I knew the actual names of the drinks my parents drank and that I knew what size bags of pot came in, how much they cost, and that joints were rolled in 'zig-zags' or that if they dipped regular cigarettes, that my brother's stole from my parents; in PCP, they were called Shermans. I didn't smoke pot, but my brothers had started down that road by this time, so I was plenty aware of pot and plenty of other drugs even if I didn't talk much. And I thought the drinks my mom and dad drank were nothing other than what moms and dads drank. Looking back, I always thought the glass cabinet was so pretty with all the fancy bottles and glasses in it.

All these topics came up during conversations with Mr. R in class when he checked in on the science program progress. This all seemed like normal stuff to talk about to me. He would ask questions while we cleaned my paint brushes at different times of the day.

Like I said, we had a normal life, and I didn't know any different.

> ***Side note:*** Since you're reading this book, you probably have some stories of being left alone, or maybe you had a special pet or imaginary friend. Maybe there was some violence in your home, on your street, or in your neighborhood that your family all had to deal with. Maybe there were just some crazy things going on around you at home. Maybe you had no home at all, or maybe things in school were different than it seemed for other kids. You

> know... we had normal lives growing up, right? That's what we thought, isn't it?

And looking back, I can see the Angels. One of them was my dog, Tramp. The other was Mr. R. At that time, they were doing what they do, and it seemed normal to me. At that time, I thought Tramp was doing what she was supposed to do by hanging out with me. And Mr. R? Doesn't every teacher teach us stuff and put things in our hands for us to learn something? Now that I'm older and can look back at the whole picture, they were giants swatting away the beasts that could have eaten me alive as I ran through the valley of good and evil. Ok… that last bit was a bit dramatic, but you get what I mean. You might have similar experiences with Angels if you think about it.

Maybe whoever it was that gave you this book is the first Angel you've met. But then again, now that I point out these giants, you might be able to name a couple more, and maybe you want to reach out to them now.

The 1st grader

As the craziness ramped up in my house, I still thought of everything as normal, I suppose. As I meet people and learn their stories, the thing we all have in common is that when we are living in the thick of life, we think everything is just normal.

At some point during my first grade in school, my family had to show up, as one unit, to court-ordered family counseling of some sort. As I write this, it occurs to me that back when I was in first grade, I understood what a 'court order' was. I knew what a 'judge' was, and I knew what 'probation officers' were. These were all words in my vocabulary by first grade. I thought this was normal stuff to have a judge require something of us. I guess I assumed all families did things like this.

I have scattered memories of what was going on in the house, but none of them are complete. It's as if the video of the memories jumps on the screen and then blips off before the end– but I have a lot of these little snippets of memories:

- I know my brothers were in trouble for things like drug dealing and breaking into houses or shops.
- They would hand their drugs to me, bottles of alcohol, or stolen things and tell me where to hide them for them as a favor.

- I know people called my parents alcoholics, and dad traveled for whatever work it was he did. I never really knew. So, we were all left to ourselves quite a bit.
- Government officials visited our house to speak with my parents about how one of my brothers had properly drawn how to build an atom bomb and sent it to the Pentagon to ask if it was correct.
- I had a sandbox out back where I liked to hang out most of the time with my dog, Tramp.
- On at least one occasion, my brothers shot out all the streetlights from our kitchen window with a .22 rifle and denied it to everyone. I never told on them ('til now). Maybe they did this more than once.
- My mom lost all her front teeth in an accident involving a window crank she ran into running up to a window and then yelling out to whoever was causing some mayhem outside our house.
- When mom and dad were gone one evening, we stacked all the mattresses from all the beds outside the second-story window and took turns jumping out onto them.
- Somehow all those mattresses got on fire…
- Somehow the bay window to the roof from my parents room was shattered and my foot was bleeding pretty badly.
- My brothers used to make up stories about illegal things going on at various houses on our street and share them on the CB radio my dad kept in his office. We would hear the sirens and go outside to watch all the action.
- And this might be the era referred to as the 'mad house' by some.

At any rate, all of that added up to why my brothers had all been put on probation and were in and out of juvenile detention centers, prompting a court-ordered family counseling session.

So, it was at one of those counseling sessions where we all met Mr. G, the social worker. Mr. G gave me a little purple dune-buggy Matchbox™ car to play with while the rest of them chatted. When the conversation got dicey or too loud for me, he would just say I could go play with the dune-buggy in the corner of the office behind his desk. I made little car noises as it raced around, and they chatted. I was only six or so, and my brothers were all eleven through fifteen years old. I didn't need to hear everything.

I was behind Mr. G's desk and apparently making plenty of racecar noise. I remember not liking the colors and shapes I saw listening to them talk, but if I made my car noise, the pretty whisps of smoke would rise in front of the shapes and shards of glass I saw, and the room would brighten. So, as I was making all the racecar sound I needed, at some point – my oldest brother called out, mixing up his words, "Yo, Dunebuggey – shut that dominic up will ya!"

It made everyone laugh, even me, lightened the mood, and the name stuck. That's what my brothers called me from then on. I have one living brother who still calls me *'Dune-Bug'* from time to time. It's our way of smiling at the past, I suppose. I love it when he calls me it.

As far as I'm concerned, Mr. G is one of my Angels. He knew what I shouldn't hear, and gave me a way to not hear it. Up to that point in my life, there was only Mr. R and Mr. G looking out for me right where and when I needed someone. And I had my dog, Tramp. At the time, I didn't understand just how significant these folks were to me. But today, they hold the biggest part of my memories.

> ***Side note:*** I'm guessing you have a Mr. G or a Mr. R somewhere around you now… or maybe you have in the past. Now that I've started sharing who my Angels are, I hope yours start coming into focus too. Knowing who they are or maybe when they were part of your life are important parts of looking back so we can add to the strength our resilience offers us.

These are some of my earliest memories. We all have early memories, and some of them might be very vivid. In fact, traumatic memories are some of the most vivid of all memories. And since all mine seemed like normal things when I was living through them, I didn't realize just how impactful they were into adulthood.

But that's not unique. It just happens to be the case for all of us who have lived through, are in the midst of, or are healing from. This is why, as you read, you will see that I am a big advocate of sharing your stories and remembering them– not to relive or reinforce any sort of victimhood. The exact opposite. You are on the other side of them now. You can take from them all the strength they afford you and be more equipped, more able, and more empowered to be the incredible person you are.

So … actually, if you do take them and make them a source of power – that is unique. Not everyone does that. I share more here about my life in the next couple sections and the last part of the book is all about the superpowers that make us, you – because of your experiences, and me – because of mine, something quite extraordinary.

As an adult ...

I'm going to pause here for just a short story on a big topic. Something that has followed me into adulthood from my early life is that I listen to everything – I hear it all. That may sound odd, but it can be a problem in some circumstances. I've also been told that it's not an uncommon phenomenon in adults with childhoods like mine, BUT, not everyone who experiences it may know just exactly what it is. So, I will share my experience. It might be that you have this same problem. Or maybe you are in the thick of life and this problem is just starting to develop for you.

Because I hear everything, there are a few places where I don't like to go and won't go if I have a choice. Any event or place that involves large crowds and the noise that comes with it is something I would just as soon avoid.

I mentioned it earlier; my home was loud most of the time, and nothing in the noise was pleasant from the very beginning. But I listened to it all. Listening is how I knew if mom or dad were drunk, or if mom was crying, or if dad was driving away. Listening was how I knew if my parents were fighting about themselves, us boys, or me or something else about the house or family. Listening is how I knew where my brothers were and what they were up to. I listened for cues to get out of the house. I heard things when I was walking back in that would tell me to stay out longer or if it was safe to sneak into bed or not. I knew from listening to everything and everyone everywhere because that's how I learned to be safe. It started in the forest for me at two years old, and I never stopped listening.

So, today, when I head into large crowds, concerts, the mall, or even a business meeting with more than a handful of people, all I hear is everyone talking, background noises like cars and sirens, even fans blowing in the window, and my brain is trying to listen to it all. All of it crashes into my ears at the same volume, and I have to really focus on the important sounds. I can't turn that off, and the noise is deafening. Maybe you have the same thing happen to you? It's real. I've just developed a trick where I can either hyperfocus my listening on one thing at a time or I simply tune out everything.

You might do the same thing. If so, some folks will be impressed with how well we listen and recall what we hear; others will think we might be hard of hearing. At the end of a noisy day, I can find myself pretty exhausted. But now a days … when I hear my wife saying, 'hey Dom…' to get my attention, I know it's time to hyperfocus my listening ☺. I call it a superpower. She knows all about it.

And I use that superpower every day, personally and professionally.

Resilient Now

Elementary School

Despite writing this book, I don't talk about my childhood very often. And when I do, I don't share details. Like most people, we say something short and sweet to get to other topics. For me, I say something like:

We moved a lot; I went to several schools growing up. I don't have too many memories but a house full of five boys was certainly crazy times.

But just like you – that's not even close to the real story. So, here's the long version:

The 2nd grader

Although I have a mental block around second grade—a few things happened then—I just can't recall them or when exactly they happened.

My oldest brother, Marty, did go to prison at some point during my 2nd grade. I know there was an event at our house to arrest him—but that's not a memory. Someone has told me what all went on that day, but I can't recall any part of it personally. I know we visited him once while he was in prison, but I can't say, exactly, when or who I was with when we visited. Even that isn't a real memory. Someone told me we visited him. I remember the name of the prison too. I remember a story about how he helped someone in prison, and he earned some sort of award. But I don't remember any of that—I think I remember eating something out of the vending machine in the waiting area in that prison. The only reason I remember that is because years later, while I was traveling abroad, I had a can of chocolate-covered ants given to me as a gift. For whatever reason, that triggered a memory. That was the thing we got out of the vending machine, and I remember eating it in the waiting room at the prison. I can't verify any of that, so I may have made up that memory as well.

So now that I've told you my oldest brother's name, I want to jump ahead in life to tell you just a little more about him. Marty passed away when he was 49 years old. He had a teenage life that led to prison. After prison, he lived a life of alcohol and drug abuse which ultimately took its toll on him. He came in and out of our lives (my wife, me, and our kids) a number of times over the course of his life. Some of those times were for longer stints of time than others. Some for happy reasons, like the birth of his daughter. Some for hard reasons, like when he came to us needing to be put into treatment for drug abuse and alcoholism (it never did stick, unfortunately). During times when we were together, I never asked him what all went down when he went away to prison, and I was just a little guy in the house. I guess we just left that in the past with plenty of other things about our family that now rest with him. God rest his soul.

That's just the short version, of course, but I will leave it there. We all know people we have lost – and their story is in our heart, right?

Jumping back to 2nd grade, I do have one solid memory. The day my dog, Tramp, died. She had been my boon companion from my earliest memory in the forest and was still the case here in Denver. After supper one evening, I took half of a meatball from my spaghetti to give to her. I did that with anything I was eating that I knew she liked too. She usually hung out in one of three places. I looked for her near my parents' bedroom door at the top of the steps. That's where she would be when we ate supper. No Tramp. I looked in my room by the closet on a blanket I kept for her there.

That's where she was when I was sleeping. No Tramp. I looked outside by the sandbox in the backyard. When I played in the sandbox, she would sit by me but stay in the grass. No Tramp. So, I called out to her once or twice. I couldn't find her anywhere. I headed back inside, and I asked my mom where she was. She was standing in the kitchen. I was just near, in the dining room. Mom didn't answer but stopped what she was doing, like she was about to answer me softly. Instead, I heard my dad's voice. He must have been standing out of view from me but within earshot when he called out that he had to have her 'put down' earlier that day, and he did say he was sorry about that. That's when I heard my mom say that Tramp went to heaven earlier that day. I didn't say anything that I remember, but I do remember handing the bowl with my half of a meatball to my mom.

And that's the end of the memory. If this were a movie, that would have been a really sad scene.

I don't have many other memories of 2nd grade. It is as if somewhere near the end of 1st grade I lost my memories, and they don't return until the winter of 3rd grade.

But before we jump to the 3rd grade, I do have a story from my adult life that ties back directly to 2nd grade that I want to share, and it's a good one!

In my married life, as an adult, at our Thanksgiving

table, a couple of my brothers joined us that year. My kids asked me if we, meaning my brothers and I, had any childhood traditions at Thanksgiving. Now, although I can't specifically recall when this happened in my childhood, I told them that my dad carved our turkey. As he was carving the bird, he would remove the wishbone and hang it above the dining room table on the chandelier. Then on the following Thanksgiving, he would take the wishbone down for the oldest person at the table and the youngest to snap the wishbone while making a wish.

Snap the old wishbone making a wish and hang the new one for next year! That's the tradition. My brothers all agreed; this was a real tradition, even though none of us could remember exactly how often or if it ever happened in our home when we were younger. If that ever did happen, it would have had to happen in our home in Denver before my oldest brother ever went away to prison. That would have been the last time we were ever together as a family, so I say it happened when I was in second grade.

Ever since I told that story to my children, it has been a tradition in our home. In fact, there is a wishbone hanging above our table right now waiting for the next Thanksgiving supper at our home. I'm hoping this tradition sticks for generations to come. What a great memory!

I've been told that things must have been pretty

bad in 2nd grade for me blank it all out – but I'm ok with that. Let's move on to third grade!

The 3rd grader

Like I said, memories blank out at the end of 1st grade, but they return when my mother, one of my brothers, the one closest to me in age, Ben, and I left the mad house. I started the 3rd grade school year in Denver and Ben would have been in 7th or 8th grade. This story is something of a miracle that happened that winter. This was the year the family split up. I shared how Marty went to prison earlier, then the next two brothers were placed in group homes in Denver, dad went off on his own someplace, and my mom, Ben, and I headed north to Grand Forks, North Dakota in the dead of winter in a little white car. I think it was a Toyota Corolla, and I'm pretty sure it was a hatchback model. I remember this story exactly as my brother remembered it as well as did our mom. We all told the same story whenever it came up:

During the storm, the driving conditions turned to a complete whiteout for my mom, driving across the county with her two youngest boys. There was no way to see the road, and we were in the middle of nowhere in the middle of the country. She had come to a stop on the road. She was crying, and my brother and I were in the backseat, looking out the back window at the storm all around us. Well, there was really nothing to see. It was nothing but dark and blowing snow.

All of a sudden, there were headlights flashing and coming close to our car. My mother saw them too in her rear-view mirror and started to inch forward. She feared it was a giant truck of some sort behind us that might hit us since they likely couldn't see our little white car. So, there we were… inching forward on the road with big headlights from a giant truck about to hit us from behind. But then, we all saw the turn signals at the same time. First, the right turn signal, and my mom veered to the right a little to stay in front of those headlights behind us. The lights followed us, and the signal turned off. The feeling was that the lights were leading us from behind. Mom straightened out the car and continued to inch forward since the big truck was still inching toward us. Then the same thing to the left. The truck signaled, and my mom veered to the left a little to stay in front of those lights. Then again, to the right, we went following the signal. All the while, the truck kept moving forward, and we kept inching forward so we wouldn't be hit.

After being 'pushed' by the headlights and guided left or right with the signals for about an hour, they turned bright and then were gone. Confused, my mom stopped the car. We were not sure what happened or where we were, except maybe further down the road. And we wondered what happened to that truck and the driver. There we sat, but only for a moment or so. A man came to my mom's door in a big coat holding a rope. He opened the door and assured all of us we were safe. He helped the three of us out of the car and into the hotel, where we had come to a stop. We came to a stop not ten feet from the hotel door that we couldn't see when the truck lights flashed and disappeared.

We asked about the truck that guided us with its lights. The man in the hotel said he didn't see anything other than our headlights coming off the road and parking in front of the door. There was no one guiding us that he saw. He asked us how in heck we could see where we were going at all off the highway and into his parking lot.

I still tear up a bit when I think of that time in our lives and that story. I don't think anyone will be able to talk me out of the idea of guardian Angels as long as I live. I've met plenty and been guided by a few over the years. I've told you about two of the Angels so far (Mr. R and Mr. G). And now you know of this Angel, who remains a mystery but is every bit as real.

The storm finally ended, and we were on our way once the roads were safe. Our travels ended for my mom and big brother when we showed up at my Grampa's house. I will never forget his hug when he saw us. Never. I don't share much about him in this book, but during high school and in college, he's been the most significant man in my life. My hope has always been to be at least half the man he was. Of all the Angels in my life, he's chief among them.

After that hug from my Grampa, my brother, my mom, and I moved into his basement apartment. I remember telling my Grampa that I could work to help pay rent since I knew my mom was going to need the help.

I think to keep me out of trouble more than anything, my Grampa introduced me to Mr. S. Mr. S owned a clothing store downtown. After school, I would check in with my Grampa at his jewelry store and with Mr. S at his clothing store. They both paid me to run errands or clean up little areas of their shops. But then, one day, Mr. S had me meet him in a warehouse he owned just around the corner from his shop. He told me he needed it swept, and he showed me how to use the big broom and spread the oiled sawdust to clean the floor. Whatever these two gentlemen paid me, it was in cash, and I gave the money to my mom. I don't think Grampa actually collected rent from us for us living there, but I'm guessing that mom used the money to help pay for our food. I know she always accepted it with a smile. I felt great giving it to her. I even felt a little pride one day when I overheard her tell someone on the telephone that I had just given her some money and that I had more than she did.

I count Mr. S as an Angel because he kept tabs on me and summoned me to work whenever I would otherwise have been alone or left to my own devices. Given the track record of my brothers, he knew what he was doing, keeping me busy and working.

> ***Side note:*** I'm not sure what track record surrounds you—but they aren't your records. You don't have to follow the path of others who walked into hell. You can see where they went, and you can choose to go another way. Maybe—just maybe, if you look around, there might be someone like Mr. S who is looking to help you walk another path... that leads to something better, or at least, away from where you know you don't want to go.

Running errands and working for this man is where I learned to provide value. I learned it because somehow, I saw it in him every time I talked to him. That mindset alone has served me the most in my entire life so far. It is the one mindset that probably kept me out of trouble and away from drugs. The reason it kept me out of trouble is because good people recognize others when all they are trying to do is add value wherever they go. Since I did the work I was told to do, and I tried to look and act like Mr. S, other people noticed and engaged in positive ways with me. I was lucky enough to be noticed.

That's what I was up to. Ben was up to other things and finding himself in trouble with school as well as the law.

Like I did with Marty, I want to jump ahead in life

to tell you just a little more about Ben. He and I grew close on our winter trip to Grand Forks. We stayed close for a number of years until our parents divorced a couple years later. Like Marty, Ben would be part of our lives (my wife and I and our kids) here and there across his short life too. Ben, too, battled drugs his whole life and developed some disturbing mental health issues even before he went into the Army. Unfortunately, our family never dealt with or even spoke about mental health or drug abuse, and so no treatment or help ever came Ben's way. He ended up dying in his late 40's, high on drugs, and in a fight where he fell down a flight of stairs. Recovery never would come from that fall. Ben was taken off life support after a short time. God rest his soul.

Before I go on here, I realize that in just a few pages, I have glossed over two lives. And a little later, I will share how I lost another brother. To be sure, they all had stories and lives of value. The tragedy is that they will never write their stories. The hurt in my heart comes from knowing a little bit about their stories... and simply living with those fragments inside me, right alongside what I know their potential was—but will never be. These are not easy feelings to deal with, and if you have similar experiences, I encourage you to find the friends and loved ones around you that you can share this with. I'm lucky. I have a beautiful family around me, and many are family by their choice, not blood. No matter—they all lift me up when I fall... or hold me steady so I don't fall from the weight of these hurts. My guess, if you have the strength and courage, you can reach out to someone who will sit beside you and hear your heart. It will do a world of good. I promise.

The 4th grader

By 4th grade, I had been in 4 or 5 schools.

If asked, I didn't make a big deal that I had moved a lot. I tried to avoid the conversation, but people ask questions of the new kid, I learned, so I had to tell everyone something, so I would say, "We move around a lot." And I would leave it at that.

In 4th grade, I had a teacher who put everyone's birthday on the calendar. If it was your birthday, we had a small party as a class. We made cards, had cupcakes, and the birthday kid got to sit in a special chair by the teacher.

I remember the first birthday party for a kid in that class. That's when the teacher showed us the party schedule with kid's names on the calendar. And then each month, she made a giant calendar with a giant wrapped box with a name on it pinned to birthday dates. It never dawned on me that my name would show up on one of the boxes. I thought that was for all the other kids, and I couldn't wait for the next party. When I saw my name pinned to a date, I couldn't believe it. In my head, I didn't really understand. How was I going to get a party like these other kids had been having in school? I thought. I had never had a birthday party. I had never been to a birthday party for anyone other than the parties in this class. I just assumed that these parties were for everyone else. I didn't ask anyone about it. I just waited to see if it was a mistake or something.

But the day for my birthday party came, and I got to sit in the special chair by the teacher like all the other kids did on their birthdays! I got cards just like everyone else had on their birthdays! In fact, I still have the cards from that party to this day; they meant that much to me. Imagine my surprise when the teacher gave me a gift just like she did with the other kids on their birthdays! Apparently, birthday gifts are a thing. Who knew? I wanted to tell everyone I knew that we should do this for everyone!

A fun side story here is that years later, I ran into one of the girls that was in that class with me. She remembered my birthday party as something more special than other birthday parties, just like I remember it. She remembered that I had never had a party before. She wrote on her card: 'you are special – Happy birthday.' I showed her the card she wrote to me since I still had it. That was a fun reunion for both of us.

But shortly after that party, we moved again. My dad came to Grand Forks and picked up my mom, my brother, and me. We headed to Arizona! I'm not sure why we moved there, but I learned it sure was hot compared to North Dakota! Once we got there, I remember asking if my oldest brother, who was in prison, and the other two, who were in group homes in Denver, knew where we were. I don't remember the answer, but I knew that none of us were close to each other anymore. And things in this apartment in Arizona were just as loud as things the last time my parents lived in the same house. There were just fewer of us living here, making the noise.

So, when I was finally enrolled in school, I remember they did some tests on me and had me speak to a bunch of people. This is when I learned that I got to go to a special room for most of the day. I thought it was because I was reading different things than the rest of the class. But as an adult reviewing my old school records, this was the beginning of the labels I dealt with, and I didn't even know it.

The first label was Emotional Behavioral Disorder (EBD). I just thought I was a good reader, and I liked doing art as well as building things or taking things apart. That special room had everything the regular classroom had, but it was a little quieter, with fewer kids, and they had a special shelf of books that I could pick from anytime I wanted. But I only had a couple months of that since it was the end of the school year.

During the summer break, we moved to Las Vegas! I'm not sure why we moved there either. All I knew was that it was just another place that was too hot!

The 5th grader

I'm not sure what happened exactly, but the label of EBD (Emotional Behavioral Disorder) that I was given late in 4th grade, back in Phoenix during the last few months of the school year, got lost when in my next school in Las Vegas labeled me GT (Gifted and Talented). I rolled with the punches. Here's how that all went down:

I showed up on the first day of class for 5th grade at the elementary school. School in Nevada then had a year-round school year, so classes started in the middle of summer. I didn't know anyone, but going to a new school was nothing new to me. I rolled with it. The first thing our teacher, Mr. H, did in class was give all of us students a series of tests to see where we all were in our schooling.

Day one, he handed out test after test: there was a spelling test, a math test, a book list check-off, and a couple questions where we had to write out our answers in essay style. A few days later, the teacher asked me to stay in his room at lunchtime to ask me a few questions. I had forgotten that I was messing around on all those tests, but it all came back to me when he asked me to stay in at lunch. I was pretty sure I was in trouble.

At this point in life, I knew Morse code and how to

write it down properly. I also knew the full phonetic alphabet used for charting how words sound versus how they are spelled. I'm not sure why I knew Morse code or the phonetic alphabet, but I did. So, for some of the words on the spelling test, I wrote the answer in Morse code using dots and dashes. For other words, I wrote them using the phonetic alphabet based on how he said the words with his accent from New Zealand.

For math, I blacked out some of the symbols in the math question and secretly changed which symbol I used instead to complete the problems. Then I wrote in tiny letters next to my answers, "What did I change?". I suppose I thought I was being funny.

For the book list check-off page, I just wrote 'yes' at the bottom. Then, I named a few main characters by some titles here and there across the page.

As I started to recall what I had done on that test day, I was pretty sure my shenanigans were going to get me into trouble.

Once all the kids were gone for lunch, the teacher came and sat across from me. He was a very large man, and I was just a little kid. His size was a little intimidating as he sat across from me. He moved desks and chairs so that he could fit in the space by my desk. Once he was seated, he grinned from ear to ear. It was a massive grin across his giant, round head. So, I smiled too. He started chuckling a little at first, and it grew into laughter as he held all my papers out in front of him. I started to laugh too, but secretly wanted to cry, knowing he was about to smash me or something. I had only met this fella a week earlier.

He asked me if I wanted to even be in his class, if I was bored, and if I wanted to do something else instead of silly tests. I just remember still being scared that I was in some big trouble. I didn't know how to answer his questions at all. He went on to explain that since I got every question asked of me wrong, that too is equal to 100% on all the tests. He said with great enjoyment and a booming voice, "You are the only student to get 100% on every test... and you worked twice as hard to make sure you got every answer wrong!" He was still laughing, but now it was a big belly laugh and very loud. But the sound I saw in my mind was different from whisps of smoke or shards of glass. It was more like a big, colorful pipe organ that was fun to look at.

When I didn't answer, he calmed himself down but remained smiling. He assured me I wasn't in trouble, so he must have figured that was what I was thinking. In fact, he had good news for me, he said. He told me that the school had some other classes in other rooms that I might like to go to instead of his classes. He told me there were different rooms in schools for Gifted and Talented students like me. Classes that could help me learn new things and learn all the things faster, and that I could learn more things than he could teach me in his class. He was just going to have my parents come in so he could talk to them about that. I knew about other rooms from my other school. I still didn't know what that meant at this school. So, I just listened and watched the pipe organ playing in my head.

I must have had a blank stare on my face since I didn't really understand anything he was saying all while trying to understand why I wasn't in trouble. He must have realized way more than I can imagine because he did something very kind, as I look back on it.

He leaned in. He put one hand on my shoulder, and his giant hand covered my entire shoulder, half my arm, and the top of his hand was against my ear. He said, "What will your parents say when they see these papers?"

I didn't answer. I didn't like the question, and I was trying to think of any other time when my parents ever saw any of my schoolwork.

"I will be sure they are as impressed by you as I am. I promise." That is what he said. I remember every word... and could write it phonetically because I remember how it sounded with his accent. I will never forget that day.

And I trusted him. I trusted the big, booming, colorful pipe organ. Somehow, I knew he was a friend. I wasn't in trouble, apparently, and he wanted to say good things about me to my parents. This was the biggest thing in my little heart at that time.

Before that meeting with my parents took place, I did go to other classrooms for GT courses after starting my day in his classroom. Things were fine, and I had forgotten that there was a meeting looming with my parents.

What I do cherish about Mr. H is how he gave me the boost of confidence I didn't even know I needed at that point in my life. That's what Angels do, I guess. When my parents came to meet him, he placed a chair just outside the door of the classroom and had me sit there while he and my parents met in the classroom.

They all went in and shut the door. I had a seat in the chair Mr. H set up for me.

I could hear the mumble of discussion through the door but couldn't always make out all the words. Not too far into the meeting, I heard Mr. H clear his throat and begin to speak much louder so I could hear every word. He said, "Your son is smart. He's been in gifted and talented classes since school began, and he is beyond 5th grade. This young man of yours is so very talented. I am sure you will see he can handle anything school throws at him and will be great at anything in life he sets his mind to. I hope you will encourage something big in him." Now imagine someone with a big, booming voice twice the size of my parents combined saying all this with a thick accent from New Zealand. Now you have a smile on your face the way I do when I recall it. That was a great day for me.

He may have said other things too... But those words rang in my head until they became something I can never forget hearing. I'm not sure how much longer the meeting went on, but when they had me come back in, they let me know that I was going to skip the rest of 5th grade and start going to 6th grade beginning that next month.

When we got back home, I was sitting on the couch, changing my socks. I don't know why, but that's what I was doing when my dad came into the room and tossed the book 'The Red Badge of Courage' on my lap. He asked if I had read it yet. The paperback he tossed on my lap was the very book I had read years earlier. I told him I had... back in the forest.

And that's all I remember about all that.

The 6th grader

As I moved into 6th grade, skipping the rest of 5th – I knew what people said about my family, and about me. Up until then, I may have heard things, but none of what I had heard ever registered in my head. In 6th grade, things started to sink in, and I guess I made a conscious decision to not care what other people said or thought about us/me.

People said things like: '… alcoholics.', '…out of control', '… broken', '…troublemakers', '…druggies', 'divorce', '… shameful', '…trash'.

And 6th grade turned out to be a violent time. My oldest brother, Marty, had just gotten out of prison in Colorado and found his way to us in Las Vegas. The next two brothers, Carl and Max, had been released as adults from foster homes and moved to Las Vegas as well. Ben and I were living in a nice trailer park in Las Vegas with our mom and dad. There was a sort of a grand family reunion at the house at one point. But it was short-lived.

At that point in time, all my brothers were into drugs (users and making money as dealers), and there were rival groups of drug dealers (to my brothers) causing some trouble in the neighborhood. There were small skirmishes every once in a while. Some required minor medical or police attention, but nothing major. We seemed to muddle on through it. From time to time, I would see each of my brothers, but only two of us officially lived with my parents in the trailer. My parents were alcoholics and rarely home. If they were asked where they were when they weren't home, my dad's answer was usually 'work' and mom usually answered, 'out'. While this was the daily status quo of our home, I was trying to figure out ways to stay at school as long as I could each day, so I wouldn't have to go home to any of this mess. Mrs. W stepped up to the plate as an Angel in my life and offered me her phone number, saying that if I needed to get out of the house, to call her. She was my 6th grade teacher. I called her more than a couple times. She always reminded me to pack some clothes for the next day and offered me a fold-out couch in a side room at her home to sleep on. She would bring me to school in the morning and drop me off where it appeared other kids were being dropped off by their parents. We never talked about it in school. I was just like the other kids who were dropped off at school.

Remember... this was the early 1980's, so times were a little different back then.

But this one night... things happened too fast. I never had a chance to make the call.

The rival dealers to my brothers pulled up in their fancy cars outside our home. They started to beat one of my brothers in the yard. My other brothers joined the fight with baseball bats to protect him. My dad happened to be home that night and left the house with his .357 magnum gun in one hand, and a bat in the other, when he saw the cars pull up. Everyone stopped fighting once dad smashed the headlights of one of the cars and pointed the gun at the leader of the pack who was beating on one of my brothers.

The dudes who pulled up in the fancy cars tried to get back in their cars, but dad smashed out all the headlights, one by one, and shot the engine of one of the two cars. The engine hissed and stopped. He pointed the gun back at the leader of the pack, who had his hands up, yelling at my dad, "… stop fu$*ing up my car!"

I remember watching my dad fly around with that bat like a Tasmanian Devil from the Looney Tunes, and then after the gun shot and that guy yelling at my dad, everything was silent. No one was moving. All my brothers were bleeding. My mom was inside the house by the front window crying silently, watching, and I was standing just outside the front door watching all of it.

It stayed like that for a few minutes, and then we could hear the sirens. The sirens came closer, finally blaring with lights around the curve to our little party. The police had arrived. Several police cars pulled up from both directions on our street. They all got out of their cars as the sirens stopped, but the lights were all still flashing red, blue, and white. They drew their guns and pointed them at my father, telling him to put his gun down. My dad never moved as the police arrived and started yelling orders, loudly. He still had his gun pointed at the leader of the pack but yelled at me to get back in the house. And once I did, I ran to the window where my mom was, still crying. She and I watched my dad put his gun on the ground next to his bat while the cops swarmed everyone still standing and took everyone to the ground, including all my brothers and my dad.

It was just me and my mom in the house that night after everyone was hauled away and the cars were towed. But we had two cop cars sitting outside our house until my dad got home. For some reason, my dad was allowed to come home only a few hours after everyone had been arrested. It might have been the first and only time I was actually happy to see him. The brother closest to me in age came home with him. He would have only been 16 at the time. But the older three were still in jail from the goings on that night, I believe. I remember being sad thinking that my oldest brother might end up back in prison after all this. This seemed like a pretty serious event to me compared to other interactions with the police and my family.

This was the last time we would have all been together this time around. About a month or two later, my mom and dad told me that they were getting a divorce. Also, along with the news of the divorce, I learned that my mom had a boyfriend, and I would be leaving with the two of them back to Denver. My brothers were all scattered in Vegas or in jail, and I learned dad had a girlfriend himself that he moved in with. This is when I started keeping some mental notes about where everyone was so we could all get back together some time, I hoped. I remember keeping a piece of paper with my dad's girlfriend's mailing address on it. I was thinking I would send a letter to him letting him know where I was and what my address was... and ask him to tell me the address of where my brothers were so I could send them letters too. I worked it all out in my head before we took off for Denver.

Ok ... I'm going to jump ahead in life again, like I did with Marty and Ben, to tell you a little more about my brother, Max. It ties directly back to this time in our family life.

He was the middle one of the five of us. Years later, in our adult lives, he surfaced for a while. He interacted for a very short time with several of us brothers and my mom. It was clear he had some mental health issues that were never dealt with, and he wasn't in control of his life. His issues drove him away, apart from all of us again. A few years later, the only thing in his pocket was a $2 bill and a business card with a phone number when he took his own life.

That phone number on the business card was mine. Max was in his late 30s and was the first of my brothers to pass away. He took his own life, jumping from a bridge, high on drugs, and losing the battle with the mental health issues that were never addressed, like all the other things our family never addressed. The police from another state called the police in my little city first. My local police came to my home to let me know. I was home alone when they came. My wife and kids were away visiting her mother. My wife was the first person I called. Next, since I knew how to get hold of our dad if I had to, I got in touch with him and let him know. That was a short call ending quickly with dad's voice cracking a bit as he said, "…gotta go…" click. Then I called my mom to tell her. That call was almost the same as the one with my dad. I would have liked to tell her in person, but the travel would have taken too long. Finally, I called my other brothers to let them know. Everyone was scattered by this time, and I think I was the only one who knew how to get ahold of everyone in their separate lives.

But about a year before all this, my wife and I had all five of us boys and my mom at our home for Thanksgiving supper. It was the last time all five of us boys and our mom had our picture taken. I keep this picture on my desk. I keep it, not as a reminder of better times for our family, mainly because that wouldn't have been true. I keep it to remind me that mental health, drug and alcohol abuse, broken hearts, mistakes, and broken families are real things. It helps me remember that everyone has a story, and there is just no way for us to know what those stories are, so kindness is a great starting point with anyone. I don't always succeed, starting with kindness, but I like to leave the house with the intent to be kind first to everyone I will see during my day. This takes work and attention.

I will share one more thing here. I was the one who sent Max away from us. My mother called and told me that Max said and did some things that were just unacceptable. Not illegal, just wrong. So, I went and found him and had him get in my car. As we drove, he asked if I was taking him to a field to beat him or kill him. I told him I was sending him back to California, where he said he came from. I bought him a train ticket and told him not to contact anyone in the family again until he got his life back together. The final thought I left him with was that when he got the help he needed, to give me a call first. I handed him $200 at the train station, his train ticket, and my business card. I sent him on his way.

I know now there are better ways to handle that, but back then, that's what I did. He never did get the help he needed, apparently.

I'm sharing all this here because prior to that Thanksgiving in our home, the five of us hadn't all been together since back in 6th grade, in Las Vegas, and that was right before my parents' divorce, not too long after the big brawl outside our front door.

So, you see, starting in 6th grade, after our parents divorced, I focused on keeping track of where my family was, so we could all get back together and be a normal family again one day.

> ***Side note:*** This was a hard section for me to write, because I was thinking of what you, the reader, might be going through.
>
> I've written about drug and alcohol abuse as something that was just a normal part of my family. If that's the case in your life, know this: These are not normal things, and they are not healthy elements of a family or personal life.
>
> Drug violence, the kind that I just described as being part of my family, or any other kind of drug violence, for that matter, is not a normal part of a life, even if this kind of violence is present in your life.
>
> Gun violence and domestic violence that were all part of my childhood are not normal for a family, even if they are part of your life today or were in your past.
>
> And because of all those things I just mentioned, this is where you and I have to understand the difference between a victim mentality and what recovery and healing look like.

> If you can relate to some of the things I mention above, and if there is a need in your life to speak to someone professionally about what you need to heal, this is my request that you seek that out now.

For me, sidestepping a victim mindset means empowerment and feels like stepping out of the shadows into the light. I've never seen myself stuck in a victim mindset, but I know what it means to be at the mercy of circumstances—the feeling of being powerless to change my situation. It was like being trapped in a dark room with no way out, feeling overwhelmed. And thankfully, I had Angels that opened doors for me to let the light shine in. I know that not everyone has those Angels... or can see them if they are there.

But what I can tell you is that an empowered mindset is just like finding the key to unlocking that door and stepping into a world of possibilities. I realize that while you and I can't change the past, we have the power to shape our future. Instead of dwelling on what happened to us, we can focus on what we can do about it. We can refuse to let our past define us, recognizing that our strength lies in our ability to rise above it.

In an empowered mindset, we take ownership of our lives and choices. We refuse to play the role of the victim, instead embracing our resilience and inner strength. We may still acknowledge the challenges we've faced, but we refuse to let them hold us back. We write our own story, and we do it with courage and determination, and hopefully with the encouragement of some helping, loving hands along the way.

Ultimately, the difference between a victim mindset and an empowered mindset lies in where we place our focus. In the former, we are consumed by past traumas and limitations. In the latter, we are driven by a sense of purpose and possibility. It's a shift from surviving to thriving, from feeling helpless to feeling empowered. And once we make that shift, we find out what success really is. I've told you what my idea of success is, and it revolves around my family today, and I have a big group I call family. What will you do?

As an adult …

Later in the book I share a number of superpowers I think I have. I'm not being silly here – Actual superpowers, that in some ways were obstacles when I was in elementary school – but developed into superpowers that fueled my resilience in adulthood. I'm taking this pause in the story to encourage you to understand something. When people like me are part of your life, or if you are someone who has had a rough go in life similar to the things I've experienced – we are all developing superpowers in our young life that will fuel resilience in our adult life.

Our experiences help us manage losing siblings, for instance. Or they help us manage past neglect in our childhood. They help us approach obstacles in life, hurdles, in creative ways. Sometimes we may just be trying to survive and wake up tomorrow. In other ways, they may develop the superpower that drives us to achieve great dreams and define success in real and important ways. And those definitions may be different than how others might define them. They are important to recognize.

As I was writing this book, I took note of those superpowers being developed and added the last section of this book to share a little more about them, for those interested. I just wanted to take a pause in telling my story, here, so you can start looking at your life and experiences so you too can start taking note of your superpowers. Maybe now is a good time to start jotting down your thoughts.

Junior High & High School

When asked how I made it through some things, one of the answers I would give was something along the lines of, 'I keep moving along...' or 'I keep moving down the road...', or '...up the hill' or '...onward and upward.' There are lots of ways to finish that sentence. I have said them all over the years. I might be the reason some of them are cliché now. Sorry about that.

Those were my short answers… here's my story:

The 7th grader

I was an inner-city kid, and I know people have called me a 'survivor' because I somehow avoided the drugs and gangs and violence that most homeless kids fell victim to in the early 1980s.

Like I've already shared– I believed I was doing OK. That's what I thought. Here's the list of things I had going for me, in my mind:

- No one knew I lived in a hotel room. They thought I had the same address as my mom in a small apartment downtown.

- The family that owned the hotel did my laundry and gave me the room if I kept the parking lot and dumpster area tidy and helped with cleaning rooms when I could.

- I wasn't on free lunch at school and was in Student Council as class president.

- I was a busboy at a restaurant after school most days, and no one had a problem with that.

- I did yard work and other chores for a lady, whom I called Ms. Havisham, on Saturdays.

- I picked up a golf caddy job on Sundays for two Rabbis at the country club.

- And finally, the Rabbis both hired me as a Shabbos goy for their homes on Friday nights, not too far from Ms. Havisham.

- Plus, I had a bike to use to get me to the Rabbi's houses and then over to do yard work.

Here's how all that came about:

Denver – again.

When mom and I left Las Vegas, I was an angry kid. I didn't understand why we were moving. I didn't know my dad had a girlfriend, but I knew her as someone he worked with. I didn't like her. I didn't know my mom had a boyfriend, and now that I did, I didn't like him. I didn't want to move back to Denver of all places, and we drove a U-Haul truck. I wasn't about to spend any time with this new guy my mom was seeing, so I opted to ride in the back of the truck. Actually, I insisted. I threatened to run away if I had to ride in the cab with those two. I know—riding in the back of a U-Haul is illegal—but I did it. Don't worry, I had a flashlight and a rock to pound on the metal bars if I had to stop to use the bathroom.

Once we got to Denver, we did all the stuff we do when moving to a new place. We got an apartment, moved our stuff in, and eventually registered for school. We generally got in the groove of a new place, and then…

Things went south for my mom and her boyfriend in just a few short months. I remember the day we were evicted from the apartment. When I walked up after school, I saw most of our stuff sitting on the lawn. A sheriff was there, stopping me from going into the apartment, and told me to just wait until the manager had taken all our stuff out—then I could get what I wanted. I'm not sure where the boyfriend went. I saw him drive off in his car when I was walking home. (To this day, I don't like classic Chevy Novas or any other of those muscle cars because that is what he drove.) My guess is he left the apartment when he saw the sheriff emptying everything out on the lawn, because I didn't see any of his stuff. My mom wasn't around right then either, and so I waited for her. I waited for all our stuff to get taken out of the apartment. When they were all done, I grabbed a duffle bag and put my things in it. I waited a little longer for my mom to show up. After a while, I realized she wasn't coming… so I left too.

Here's the thing: This is when I was in 7th grade back in Denver, where we all lived when our family broke up the first time. My brothers had made a reputation for the family name in the school system and in that neighborhood, and I didn't want any part of that trouble. I was even president of the student council for my class, probably trying to overcompensate or something for what our family reputation was. I was a decent student and was even on the football and wrestling teams.

In the few months I had been in school, I had made a few friends, and they knew my home life was a little shaky. I had one friend whose family owned a restaurant. Since they knew my situation, they had me work at the restaurant as a busboy after school to earn money and a free meal with every shift. Most nights after school, I could take the public bus within a block of the restaurant.

And I had another friend whose family owned a motel. This is the kind of motel on a busy road with an apartment attached to it for the owner/family to live in and run the hotel from there. That's where my friend lived, and her family offered me a room if I would help keep the parking lot and dumpster areas clean each night when I got there. And they would have me help clean the room when they moved me around from time to time.

Homeless

The night I left the apartment where we had been evicted, I took that family up on their offer to stay at the motel. I didn't bus tables that night since I had to figure out where I was going to sleep that night. I went with my best bet and headed to the hotel my friend's family owned. I started by cleaning the dumpster area before I went into the office and asked them for a room that night while my mom sorted out where we were going to live. I had supper with them that night, and they gave me a hotel room and my own key. I'm not sure where my mom went that night, or, really, I didn't know for a while. Eventually she found another boyfriend, and they had a small apartment downtown. So, I stayed in the hotel, cleaning the dumpster area each night after bussing tables.

Everything was working out just fine as far as living arrangements went, I thought. But then, one day, on Student Council Day, I was called into the office. I didn't think anything of it since it probably had to do with Student Council. But that's not what the meeting was about. In the principal's office were a few other people, and I recognized one of them as the nice lunch lady. The principal explained that they had checked on our new address and had spoken on the phone to my mother, but she didn't want to talk to them. That's why they had me in the office. They said that they had programs for families like mine with limited money. The lunch lady started talking about the free lunch tickets. The other lady started talking about clothing stores I could go to for free or reduced-cost clothes, but complimented how well I was dressed. They wanted to know if there was enough room for me in the apartment my mom gave them as my address, where she lived.

When there was a pause in all the talking, I realized

I wasn't in trouble! And they didn't know I lived at the hotel, and they didn't know I worked at a restaurant that shuffled folks from Mexico into the country through the kitchen help, which I swore to keep secret. They just thought I was a poor kid who lived in a tiny apartment with his mom and her new boyfriend. Perfect!

So, I said, "It's small, but we all have enough room. I think those striped tickets are for the poor kids in school. We are doing just fine. I buy my lunch tickets every Monday like everyone else." She had already complimented what I was wearing, so I didn't think I needed to say anything about the low-cost clothing store.

The principal asked who gave me the money to buy my lunch tickets. I told him my mom did. He asked who washed my clothes for me. I told him my mom did. He asked if there was a clean bed for me in that apartment. I said yes and added that I had a blue blanket (but I didn't). He asked if there was food at the house, and I told him my mom made spaghetti most nights and fresh bread all the time, which was a lie. (The last time she made spaghetti or bread was back when we lived in Denver the first time around.) I told him I ate an apple or banana every day after school, waiting for supper (but that was a lie since I looked forward to a free meal after bussing tables each night at the restaurant when I worked). The caddy master had oranges for me when I showed up on Sundays (more about my caddy career later ☺). I'm not sure why I picked an apple and a banana to lie about. Maybe because sometimes back in the forest we had those around.

They asked if I needed anything. I said I couldn't think of anything. And then I tried to change the subject, saying, "I thought I was called to the office about Student Council things."

It wasn't a question. But it seemed to work. They stopped asking questions like I hoped. The room was silent, and everyone just looked around at each other. The lunch lady tried to hand me the striped tickets (the free lunch tickets had a red stripe down the middle). I said I didn't need any, but I thanked her for offering them to me. The principal just smiled and said, "OK. We will see you at Student Council later."

Work

I don't remember what day that was, but I remember that my mom worked at a dry cleaner near the apartment she lived in with her boyfriend. I went to visit her after school that day, and to tell her everything I told the school people, so if they checked, she would know what I said. During the visit, I noticed that she wasn't wearing any of her pretty rings. My Grampa (her dad) was a jeweler. My dad also made jewelry as a sort of hobby, and my mom always had pretty jewelry. But that day, she didn't have any on her hands. I asked her where the rings were. It was just her and me in the store, and she began to cry. She told me that she had to sell them. She needed the money. I sat with her, and she explained how pawnshops buy things like that and that she sold them to the one just down the block three days earlier. She said they would still be there if she did get the money to buy them back, but after a week, they would sell them.

A customer came in and interrupted us. Mom cheered up quickly to greet the customer and get back to work. I went out the back door by the break room, where my mom's purse and a coffee pot sat on a single table with a single red vinyl chair. I propped the door open with a wire clothes hanger and headed back to my hotel room. I grabbed all my money that I kept in a shoe with all my other clothes in a duffle bag under the bed, and I headed to the pawnshop. I didn't have any other work that day, so I had time.

The guy at the pawnshop said that he only had three of her rings left. The others were all sold. I didn't think that sounded right based on what my mom told me about how these places worked, but I didn't know how to argue with him. This was my first time in a pawnshop. But I bought the three rings he had that belonged to my mom. I went back to the propped door at the dry cleaners, went in, and put the rings in my mom's purse with the rest of the money I had.

As I was doing that, an old, strange-looking lady

dressed all in white with sunglasses came in and asked what I was doing. I told her I was just visiting my mom and waiting back in this room for her. She called my mom back, and mom told her it was true. My mom then introduced me to the woman dressed all in white as the owner of the dry cleaner shop. I don't remember her name, but she reminded me of someone… I just couldn't put my finger on it right then. But then the lady said that she was on her way home and asked if I would like to "earn a few bucks" and help her with the leaves in her yard. I said yes and stood up, ready to go!

She had a white sheet covering the back seat of her car, where she told me to sit. She told me to stay on the sheet. I did, and I didn't really see any other way to sit. We drove to her house. To me, it looked like a mansion with a big iron fence all around the yard. The gate opened all by itself, and the yard had a fair amount of leaves and other debris around. There was a rake and bags ready, sitting by the garage door. She parked and showed me around the yard, pointing to where she wanted me to pick up the leaves first. Once she went inside, I got busy.

When I was done, she waved me into the house through the back door. When I entered, I was standing in what seemed like a giant pantry, a lot like at the restaurant, but without much food in it. She had me follow her out of that room, through a large kitchen, and into a little room with a small desk where she opened a box and started going through paperwork, or envelopes, or something.

While I watched her, I looked around and could see through two different doors leading to big rooms. Everything in each room was covered in big white sheets. And then it hit me—she reminded me of Ms. Havisham from Great Expectations (a great book if you haven't read it). She looked how I imagined Ms. Havisham looking when I read the book, and I must have been chuckling a little.

Without looking up from her box, she asked, "What are you laughing at? You seem to be a pretty happy little boy for no good reason."

I remember those words exactly because I didn't understand what the comment meant. Maybe I still don't understand, but as an adult, they sound like an insult. They didn't sound like one when I was standing there. I just shrugged my shoulders and thanked her for letting me pick up the leaves.

"Oh no, no, no... you aren't done." She stood up and handed me some money that I just put in my pocket when she told me to follow her. We went out yet another door, and she pointed to a bike leaning against a fence.

She asked if I had a bike. I told her I didn't. She asked if I knew how to ride one. I said I did.

She said she knew where my mother and I lived and asked if I knew how to get back home from her house. I said I did, but I didn't, and I wasn't sure if she meant where my mom lived or where I lived at the motel. And I hadn't paid any attention to where she was driving when we drove to her house. I was lost.

She said I could use the bike if I wanted to come back during all my free time to pick up the rest of the leaves and do other chores. And she said she would pay me like she had that day. I told her I would come every Saturday morning and more often if I could. I put out my hand to shake on it. That's when she chuckled a little. We shook on it, and I jumped on the bike to figure out where the heck I was.

Caddy

Before all this, when my mom got her job at the dry cleaner, she told me that some of the people who dropped off their clothes were golfers on the weekend. It was just small talk about golfing, caddies, carts, and the restaurant at the clubhouse. I was curious about what a caddy was. That seemed like something I could do. How hard could it be to haul a bag of golf clubs around? I looked on a map and learned that the golf club wasn't too far, and I could get almost a block away from it using the city bus. So, one Saturday, I headed to the golf course in my best clothes before the sun came up. I was there before there was much going on, and I saw a guy driving carts out of a garage and parking them in a row. I watched him for a while. Once he noticed me, he waved me over and asked if I wanted to help him out. He showed me how to unplug the carts and told me if I was around later, I could help him plug them in again when people were done using them. I hung out there all day. At some point, he asked where my parents were and if I was golfing with them that day. For whatever reason, I told him the truth. I said I didn't have any parents there. I told him it was my first time at the golf course, and I was there to see if I could work as a caddy, but I didn't know anything about it.

The short story here is that after he asked a few more questions and got more truth out of me than I wanted, he made up a great story. He was a young guy and was all in to help me out. He and I walked over to the building where caddies start their day, and then he lied, introducing me to the caddy master as Mr. and Mrs. So&so's nephew, and then told him that I wanted to learn how to be a caddy. The caddy master told me to come back on Sunday morning, and he would give me some lessons.

I was in! I showed up Sunday morning like he told me to. As he was explaining things, two gentlemen who were picking up their bags learned I was some big shot's nephew learning to be a caddy. They said they would give me a shot and some pointers if I wanted to caddy for them. I agreed, and that's when I met the two Rabbis. I learned to double caddy for these two guys with the bags on the back of a cart for some, but not all, of the day golfing. After a few Sundays, the real story of who I was came out, and they asked if I would like to do some sacred work for them and their families.

As long as I lived in Denver, I worked for them on their Sabbath, or Friday nights to me. And I caddied for them on Sundays. So, when Ms. Havisham gave me a bike to get around between their houses and hers and my hotel, I was one happy kid. I think that's why her comment about me 'having no good reason to be happy' struck me. I was pretty happy with all the arrangements:

- Bus boy most nights (free meal after work).
- Work for the Rabbi's on Friday night (free leftovers).
- Yard work for Ms. Havisham on Saturday.
- Caddy for the Rabbis on Sunday.
- Everyone paid me in cash. I bought all my own stuff and lunch tickets… and I could sneak money into my mom's purse from time to time!

Perfect. I had it better than everyone, I thought.

~ ------------ ~

Everything falls apart …

My mom and her boyfriend got mixed up in a cult-like spiritual group. Actually, I think that's where she met this guy in the first place. Not a dangerous cult—

just a whacky group that had strange ideas about who they were in relation to God. Mom pulled me in too. She said it would be good for our family, and I actually enjoyed a lot of it—most of it, really. It wasn't all bad. This cult had 'fellowships' that helped out those in their local group. It was through this group that she and her boyfriend found some steady work as painters. And it was her 'fellowship' that helped them get out of their tiny downtown apartment and into a small twin-home in a better part of town. And I moved into that home with them, out of the hotel. And we had juice and milk delivered to the front door! Things were normal again, I guess.

But the drinking didn't stop. It just got worse, really. He and my mom would both drink, and he would become angry and enraged in that house at all hours. He would blame my mom for things. He would blame me for things including eating his food and drinking his orange juice and costing him too much and being a burden on my mother, blah, blah, blah. All normal stuff in every home I had lived in. I never felt as though anyone would have ever hit me or thrown something at me, but with him, I always felt he might. And as his rages grew, they got louder and louder... and, well, I don't like loud.

I kept it together for school and student council by mostly not going home unless I had to and then only late at night after bussing tables and a late supper at the restaurant.

But one night, he was up late waiting for me when I got home. The whole house was dark when I was sneaking into my room quietly. When he spoke, it startled me. Usually, no one was awake when I got home. He had a bottle on the table in front of him, and his glass was still half full, but the bottle was almost empty. He asked where I was all the time when I wasn't home. I told him I was at school or working. He asked where I worked, and I told him that I worked at a restaurant, but I didn't tell him which one. He wanted to see my money. I lied, saying I spent it all and didn't have any. He asked who was buying my clothes. I told him I was, and that's what I spent my money on. He accused me of stealing my clothes. I stayed silent; it wasn't true, and he was getting louder. I really did buy my own clothes. The interesting thing is that this was the longest conversation I had ever had with him, and I wanted it to be done quickly.

Then he showed me a shirt and asked where I got it. I told him I had never seen that shirt before in my life—and besides that, it was huge. It wouldn't even fit me. His voice turned into complete rage, and he accused me of stealing his shirt and hiding it from him in my room as he waved that shirt in my face. He kept yelling that he found it in my room and demanded to know why I was stealing his clothes if I made so much money. Usually, when things were this loud, the dark colors and sharp shapes filled my head—but not this time. This time was different. My head was clear, and my eyes were focused on him like I had never focused before.

I told him I hadn't done that, and I stepped back, but now I was against a wall. He was drunk and really angry, and I thought I was going to be in a fight with a man three times my size. But I didn't care. As he stepped towards me, I pushed away from the wall because I thought, 'This is it—the fight is on.'

I said his name out loud as I pushed off from the wall, which seemed to make him snap out of his rage for a split second. It was dark, but I knew he was staring at me. What little light there was shined in through the window from the moon or streetlight and fell on my face, so I knew he could see my eyes when I looked at him. I said, "You can try to beat me up right now if you like—but if you ever touch my mom, I will kill you."

> ***Side note:*** Looking back at that moment, it breaks my heart to think any teenager would have to say such words, let alone have it in his or her heart and mind to believe it to be true—and ready to actually fight like that. And I know that there are people who will read this book who have had to harbor things in their hearts much worse than this, at even a much younger age, and maybe even more often than I did. It's for these reasons that I am writing this book.

> That is the sort of thing that needs to have a place to heal. Had I recognized the Angels around me growing up at the time, healing might have come sooner. But it took me until I was an adult with my own kids and a loving wife to look back and see just how powerful my Angels were in my life. My prayer is that you can find yours sooner than I recognized mine.

After I said those words, he stopped. I know he was staring at me, but I don't think he intended to fight me anymore. He finally turned and walked out of the room. I'm not sure what made things stop so abruptly, but it did. I stood there for a couple minutes, listening to see where he was going or what he was doing. All he did was head back up the steps to his room. I went to my room and packed my duffle bag. The next morning, I left. I hoped my mom would be okay.

The 8th grader

There is a phenomenon in business and in life called the 'hockey stick effect'. Big changes mean things tend to decline or go down for a little bit to adjust to that big change and then pivot sharply up for a sustained period, like the shape of a hockey stick.

That's what happened here a little bit in my life.

> ***Side note:*** early on in this book, I shared my hitchhiking adventure. Here is the rest of that story, including why I was heading to Grand Forks in the first place.

After I had that encounter with my mom's boyfriend, I headed to my room and packed my duffle bag. I was tired. I knew the monster had most likely passed out in bed. I figured I could take a little nap before I headed out the next morning. As I drifted off to sleep, I made plans to not just leave the house in the morning. I had it in my head to go back to my Grampa's house. I knew it was far away, but I knew my brothers hitchhiked to various places. I thought I would give that a try.

In the morning, I was up much earlier than normal and before the sun was up. I returned the bike to Ms. Havisham, leaving it right where I found it when she offered it to me. And then I headed out. I pulled out the maps I had been holding on to for years and studied the path from Denver, Colorado, to Grand Forks, North Dakota. Whooo hoo. This was a grand adventure.

> ***Side note:*** Back in the winter of 3rd grade, I kept all the maps my mom marked up with a path from Denver to Grand Forks. I guess I thought they were cool. She used a red felt tip marker and a blue ink pen for notes here and there. These were the maps I dug out from the bottom of my gym duffle bag.

If anyone takes this trip by car today, they will plan for a 14-hour car ride. It took me four and a half days of hitchhiking and making up stories and trying to figure out how to eat. During my four-plus-day trek, I slept behind roadside rest buildings or gas stations where no one would see me. When the people who picked me up from the side of the road where I stood with my duffle bag and thumb out, I was all smiles. They asked all the questions you might expect: Is everything OK? Do you need any help? Where are you headed? Are you alone?

I lied. I lied to every single person and to every single question they asked me, and I told some whoppers:

"I'm just heading to the next town." And I would flash a glimpse of the map folded so that the next town was visible.

... and then I would explain with another lie, "It's a big challenge. My brother and I are racing each other. He started in the next town and is hitchhiking back to this town. I'm hitchhiking from this town to the next one. We have to call each other on these payphones to see who wins." I had a fake phone number on a sheet of paper, and when I told this lie, I would show them the piece of paper to really sell the 'big challenge'. I would just name the right cities, and I would smile with real excitement to encourage them to hurry so I would win the race. Since this was my go-to lie, I had to stop at almost every town along the way.

Or, other times, depending on the situation, I would say, "My brother is driving the car to the next town, but it's having some trouble, so I'm hitchhiking back home to tell our uncle, who's a mechanic, where he's driving it to."

When we would get to the next town, I would have them just drop me off 'where my aunt worked as a teller'. Or... 'over at that one, where my uncle worked.' And I would point to the shop from the highway.

At one point, the woman insisted she drop me off at my uncle's house, which I lied about. She was the first to throw a wrench into the lies. I was nervous, but I didn't show it. I was about to get caught in my lies as I pointed out my uncle's house. I just picked a random house and started making plans to run fast when it didn't work out.

I knocked on the door. An older guy with thick

glasses opened the door and was holding his wallet, and for some reason he said, "Ok, come on in." and he opened the door wide for me to step past him. I turned to the driver and waved her off, stepping into the man's home. I stood there, looking at him. He closed the door, turned, and looked at me. I think he was waiting for me to talk first, but I didn't know what he wanted me to say. I could see through the window that the lady who drove me to the house was driving away. He finally said to me, 'Ok? How much will it be?" and had his wallet at the ready. Playing along, I said, "For what, sir?"

He seemed both amused and a little impatient. "For the new subscription? How much will the paper cost me now?" He asked like he was ready to talk business with me.

I caught on immediately. He thought I was the paperboy! He wanted to pay his bill and thought I was there to collect it. I had a friend back in Denver who was a real paperboy, and I went with him when he collected money from his route, so I knew what this all about. Playing right along and without missing a beat, I said, "Oh – yes. Of course! Well, hold on." I unzipped my duffle bag just a little bit and looked inside. I was trying to make it look like I was ready to talk business too, and I had important stuff in my bag.

"Shoot. Sir… You are the first house I am stopping at, and I forgot my paper book. I'm really sorry about that." Then I turned and looked out the side window of the door to make sure the car was really gone, then I turned back to him, "My mom just dropped me off. Let me walk home and get my book, and I will rush right back. I'm really sorry about this." I thought he bought it, but I wasn't sure.

He laughed. He told me he would be here and that he loved the paper or something like that. I wasn't really listening at that point and just wanted out of the house. What I remember most is that my heart was ready to burst from my chest, almost getting caught. He opened the door, and I couldn't walk away fast enough. I may have even started running.

Other than the paperboy lie to the fella with the thick glasses, I never had a heart-pounding moment. No one ever questioned any of my lies. Most people thought whatever my lie was, was either cute, helpful, or dangerous. I would agree with them, whatever they thought. There was no harm in agreeing with any of those responses.

My last ride was from just north of Fargo to Grand Forks. I told the driver who picked me up that I was heading back to Grand Forks. I said that my mom was having car trouble in Fargo, and I was going back to Grand Forks to let my Grampa know so he could come back and help her out. The first driver I lied to using that story offered to drive me all the way back to my Grampa's house. Good thing I was actually headed to his house this time. I gave the driver the address and told him how to get there from the highway. I felt like I almost hadn't lied to this guy. The driver dropped me off in the driveway, and I waved him off as I stood at the first step up to the porch. He didn't leave. So, I walked up the steps.

Once I was at the door, everything else in my head went blank. I couldn't see anything other than the doorway. It was like the whole world turned to thin air, and all that was left was a single screen door in front of a wooden door with a doorbell just to the side. I pushed the button and everything else faded away.

My Grampa opened the door. I snapped out of whatever trance I was in and turned to wave the driver off and turned back to face my Grampa. He simply said, "Dominic. Come to me." and he held out his arms for the most important hug I had ever had in my life up to that point.

~ ------------ ~

I can tell you that there were plenty of folks surprised to see me when I got to Grand Forks. The official story I put together for everyone in Grand Forks that asked was: 'A friend of ours from Denver drove me. And I lied, saying that we drove straight through, only taking a day and a half. And then I sort of told the truth, saying that mom was okay but couldn't take care of me anymore, so a friend offered to drive me to Grand Forks; that was why I was there. And I added that my mom might come too one day. That was the lie I told, but then that last bit about my mom coming too became true. Grampa let me know my mom and her boyfriend were on their way. My guess is that someone probably gave my mom a call.

Even with that bit of bad news, a lot of wonderful things happened despite the boyfriend showing up with my mom in Grand Forks.

Here's the list of all the goodness:

An uncle took me to a dentist. When I went, I couldn't recall the last time I had been to a dentist. That was just the beginning of the Angel he was in my life.

My cousins. I fit right in with my aunt and uncle's family. Although they are technically cousins, we count ourselves much closer than that. They call me their little brother, and they are absolutely my big sisters in our gown-up lives. My uncle (their dad) comes to my wife's and my home for his birthdays, and we make it a family reunion with a giant, dangerous bonfire every year now. What this family gave me when I was a lost little kid back then is priceless.

An aunt got me some new clothes, a haircut, and a Dr. visit. I couldn't remember the last time I had been shopping with anyone. More than that, I couldn't remember the last time anyone else paid for my clothes! And apart from one medical emergency in 6th grade, I couldn't remember any other Dr. visits up until then in my entire life. To this day, this aunt sends me birthday, Christmas, and Easter cards. She's been to my current adult home, and her smile from ear to ear is enough for me to know who the Angels are in my life. I know I've surprised her by how things have turned out, but I have surprised myself, so she's not alone.

And I met a wonderful family who treated me like one of their own. A real family. A mom. A dad. A brother and a sister. They lived in a house and had an extra room they made mine. We laughed and prayed together. We ate meals together at a table. The three of us kids stayed up late watching TV and falling asleep together on a couch. And they are the ones who saw me through high school and planted dreams of college in my head. They couldn't be more real to me as a family than my own brothers are. Today, my kids call them Gramma and Pop. My little brother is a terrific uncle who hung out with my daughters in Europe when they visited him. My little sister is jealous that I'm a Grampa first. But she has a beautiful family herself, and she will catch up to me… one day. Her kids call me uncle. This is the stuff of life.

All those people jumped in. They walked with me and never said a word about who did what, or what was wrong or what wasn't working. They never talked about blame. They never did anything other than meet me in the thick of it and walk with me, leading me to a better place. Angels. All of them.

And to top all that, at school, they really welcomed the new kid (me). The Jr. High learned I was in student council in Denver and put me on the council there, too, right away. No election; I was just on the council, and everyone was happy to have me. Great stuff all the way around.

But... in the midst of all that goodness, we had to deal with that boyfriend living in my Grampa's house.

Once mom and that guy got to Grand Forks, they started abusing my Grampa's home, where they lived. The boyfriend started raging, drunk, in that house, like he did back in Denver. And while I was at my other family's home, I got a call from my Grampa that I better come. The boyfriend had hit my mom in his rage and locked himself in the bedroom.

I was just over a half-mile away and sprinted. The entire sprint, I replayed what I told him in Denver, and I was going to make good on that promise. I showed up in record time, and Grampa said the boyfriend was locked in the bedroom and that the cops had already been called.

I told myself to work fast—I had to take care of this before the cops got there because I knew all they would do was arrest him at the very worst. I went to the door and told him to get out. I reminded him through the door of the promise I made back in Denver, and I think my Grampa overheard me. I looked over my shoulder, seeing my mom sitting in a chair being tended to by my Grampa and an aunty that happened to be there.

The drunk, raging fool boomed out of that room and passed me heading to the door, snarling curse words and threats at me all the while. I had forgotten how big he was. It was just something I noticed but wasn't scared by. As I followed him out of the house, I grabbed the bat by my Grampas door and stepped out after him. He turned towards me, and I cracked him one with everything I had, aiming for his head but connecting with his shoulder and neck. He turned fully around, spinning in a daze, and when I saw his face again, I slammed the butt of the bat square against his nose, smashing his face. He was falling to the ground, where I intended to end it for him. I turned to grab the bat I lost from the last blow, and when I turned back to him, I saw him scrambling into some bushes holding his face. I could also see the trail of blood on the grass and sidewalk.

The cops pulled up just as I was walking to the bush where that idiot was hiding. My Grampa took my shoulders and turned me around towards him into a hug. He didn't let go. Neighbors came out and pointed the cops to the coward in the bushes.

The bloodied fool emerged and told the cops he wanted to press charges against me. I heard the cops say something along the lines of, 'For what? Looks like you fell on your face. What a shame.' I was angry with myself for failing in my mission. My Grampa just kept holding me.

    That was the last I heard of my mom's boyfriend. I went back into my Grampa's house to check on my mom once he was taken away.

The 9th grader

After that incident with my mom's boyfriend in 8th grade, my uncle introduced me to a fella who owned a gym for training boxers. The fella invited me to come down and see. So, I did. This was something that seemed interesting. It was a great match for me at the time. I stayed in boxing from then on through high school.

I was nothing outstanding as a boxer or athlete—but it was a great place for me to be. Since I'm telling my stories, here's a good one: My mom had never been to any boxing match of mine. I finally convinced her to come to one early on in my boxing career, and I was pretty excited that she was ringside. Excited, because up until this point in life, no member of my family had ever seen anything I had ever done or been in. Not anything in theatre, no boxing matches, no school events, or awards. This was big to me. Mom was in the house!

The bell rang for round one of a three-round match. I threw the first punch and missed. The second punch came from my opponent and landed as perfectly square on my nose as it could. My face exploded in blood as I fell to the mat. Two punches had been thrown, and I was on the mat looking around for my mom. I saw she had left her seat, but I caught a glimpse of her walking down the aisle and out the doors of the arena. I guess that wasn't the best match to convince her to come to ☺.

I'm sharing about my boxing experience because, as we already know, my uncle is an Angel, but the boxing coach was too. He knew I wasn't a boxer. I'm not overly athletic and never have been. But he also knew why my uncle sent me in there to meet him. This guy, this coach, taught me way more than boxing. He taught me to deal with anger in a very different way than how my mom's boyfriend dealt with it. Plus, the way that I dealt with that man wasn't the healthiest thing either. I did have a mindset to kill him, and I felt I failed myself, hoping to have another shot at it sometime in life. Coach helped me come to terms with the idea that my failing to do what I planned to do to my mom's boyfriend was a good thing. He explained that there was more in store for my life than what prison would offer if I killed a man. And he helped me understand that. He took the time to learn everything else that had gone on in my life, and he knew about my brother's track record—and my family life. He was a good man. He was a hard man. He taught me hard things in a strong way, and at the time, I just called him coach.

Today, I call him an Angel. My tough Angel who taught me what fighting for something we care about or protecting those we love, really means. I have many debts to pay in life that I will never be able to repay—

and one is to him.

When 9th grade rolled around, I started working again. I had it in my head that I was going to go to college. 9th grade was the last year in Jr. High school, and then 10-12 was at the high school. Two buddies and I applied as busboys at a family restaurant near the high school. We figured we could work there all summer and walk there after school once we were in high school.

So, I did that. I worked in that restaurant all through high school.

Although we started out as busboys, over the course of high school, I was also a dishwasher, prep cook, and kitchen cook. The owner of the restaurant let me know that he thought I could be head cook and wanted me to start working with the kitchen manager so I could help manage the kitchen too. Mr. B was his name, and I remember the day when he told me of his confidence in me. That was an important day for me, personally.

I'm telling you about my job as a cook because the owner saw something in me and pushed me to go further than I would have if simply left to myself. I thought I just needed a paycheck. He taught me that was the smallest thing I was earning. Along with Coach, these two men told me to 'keep moving...' and gave me healthy tools to do it right. I'm pretty sure I was the youngest head cook he ever had, and I was a full-time high schooler on top of it. He shifted things around to let me come in earlier than school and do my assistant kitchen manager work; head to school; come back later at night to cook the night rush and prep schedules for the next day.

But I had to be willing to do that work, and I was. I know people will read this book and think about the child labor laws and all the rules these folks were breaking by having me work how I worked... all the way back to Denver. My hope is that you look past all that since none of it is the point or matters at all. There was something bigger going on, and, in this case, Mr. B was an Angel in my life. The point is that when we are active—and doing something that engages our life and our mind and our heart, like work—our path in front of us narrows. It narrows in a good way, pushing all the paths of destruction way to the peripheral, harder to get to. The paths that become most available to us are those that don't lead to hell. They lead to... just better. Or maybe they provide a path away from hell. Either way, those are the paths we want in front of us, and Mr. B is an Angel for shining a light on all the right paths for me that come from doing good, honest work.

When I was getting close to graduation from high school, I shared my plans for college with him. He was the first to write me a check and call it a scholarship when I finally told him I was moving since I was accepted at a university. Not only did he give me a scholarship, but he also offered me a job—whatever hours I could work—at a restaurant he owned in my college town. I took him up on that offer and was a cook for my first two years in college as well, still working for him. After that, I worked full-time in my college theatre until I graduated. He was an Angel of mine, and I will never forget his name.

10th-12th grade

Just like back in 6th grade, I knew what people said about me and my family. Especially after the altercation with my mom's old boyfriend:

"Following in his brother's footsteps ..."

What I knew is that despite all of that, my teachers were rooting for me. They would make sure I was on time to work and play practice or whatever sport I was trying to be part of.

10th through 12th grade was the longest I had ever been in one school, in one town, in one place. I was graduating from high school with friends I had made in 9th grade! Amazing stuff.

Somewhere early in high school, the prospect of going to college came up and excited me. I now had goals for saving my money instead of just using it to survive. But even more exciting was the idea that I would actually graduate from high school. That would be a first for our family. Even my brothers were excited that someone would be able to do that among the five of us, finally.

These two very large goals of graduating high school AND going to college came about because of two incredible teachers. And a third, who almost ruined all of it.

In high school English class, it began with a reading list of books and classics. I had already read all of them on the list, so I asked the teacher what happens next. "Can I just write book reports and skip class?" I asked.

They pushed me up to American and Classical Literature intended for the senior class. I had already read almost everything the class was going to cover, including everything by Shakespeare. The teacher asked me to head to the library and find 25 books that I haven't read. He asked that I include, in my search, a number of authors I hadn't heard of. All of them were playwrights, and the only playwright I knew by name was Shakespeare at that point. His list included Sam Shepperd, Arthur Miller, Oscar Hammerstein, Tennessee Williams, and Lillian Hellman (all playwrights and authors you should read if you haven't yet).

The short story here is that I fell in love with theatre. I hadn't read anything by any of those authors yet. This teacher showed me the theatre where these plays had been staged by the drama department. Back in class, he had me write a couple plays myself and design the sets for them as well. Then he had me learn how to run the theatre lights and sound system and build props, and he had me join the drama club to build sets and act as a student director for the theatre department.

I'm sharing this because getting involved in theatre, boxing, track, or sports of any kind all grabs your mind and pushes other things, dangerous things further away from possible paths to take. As an adult, I have endless hobbies for the same purpose. Stay busy with things you love. I have to give this teacher credit for showing me something bigger than myself, where I grew, learned, and my world expanded.

And then there was the guidance counselor. He was a great man. I won't share all the stories of why I have such admiration for this fella, but when I told him I was going to college, he was instantly certain of two things. I told him I was thinking about Theatre as a major. The first certainty he told me was that he believed I would be outstanding and that I would likely not end up in theatre as a career or where I would find happiness in life. The second certainty he shared was that I would find my happiness once I had a family to care for, and it wouldn't matter what my career was. So, he signed off on Theatre as a pursuit and helped me apply to universities. If ever there was someone so right, it was him. I count Big G an Angel for more reasons than just that.

I'm sharing my stories about these two high school teachers because they had profound impacts on my life, but at the time, I didn't know it. I encourage you to look at those gems of people in your life who you remember by name. You remember their name for a reason. Think of those names you remember with fondness and think about why. Think of the impact they have had on your life. These people are Angels… and they didn't even know it. But you do now, just like I do. These are the memories to cherish. Toss the others. The memories you toss don't make life better, so you won't be losing anything important.

Then there was this other teacher. One of my high school teachers had become my friend and a trusted confidant who knew more than any other teacher about my life. The summer I moved to college, I was back visiting during an early break just after moving onto campus. He suggested we go fishing as a sort of congratulations for my heading off to college.

On the first day of our trip, we got to our hotel rooms and got our fishing gear all set for the morning. We cracked open a couple bottles and had some drinks, toasting my future. That night, he tried to sexually molest me in my hotel room. I was not a student any longer. I was older than 18. I guess he thought he was in the clear about this being a problem.

I'm sharing this story for only one reason. My boxing coach had helped me understand how fortunate I was that I hadn't killed my mother's boyfriend with a bat just a few years earlier. That rage welled up in me again that night when this trusted teacher came on to me in the middle of the night after we had both been drinking and celebrating a real triumph in my life.

Like I said, he probably thought this wasn't going to be a problem. He was wrong.

I woke up as soon as he climbed into my bed. It proved to be his worst mistake. And when I was done proving to be a mistake on his part, I cleaned the blood off my hands and changed my clothes. I left in the middle of the night and hitchhiked back to my dorm. I called my adopted dad from the dorm room phone, the man my kids call Pop today, and I told him what happened and that I thought I had killed that teacher in that hotel room.

He told me to stay where I was. And I did. I was in my empty dorm room and thought about how all my hopes and dreams for the future were going down the drain. The youngest of the five boys was now on his way to jail, like the rest. The coach warned me. He taught me better than this. I didn't want to talk to my boxing coach. I didn't want to talk to anyone. I had failed, and I knew better.

Pop showed up at my dorm but didn't have any police with him. I had prepared myself for talking to the police and was ready to take responsibility for what I did. I was going to tell them everything that happened, knowing it wouldn't matter. I knew this teacher's family very well, and this story just wouldn't be good for any of them. And as I lay thinking about all these things, I even wrote a note to my roommate, one of my high school classmates, who knew this teacher as well as I did. I knew when he got back to start college, he would see the note instead of me, and the stories would begin...

Pop is a gentle, caring man. All he has ever been capable of is caring for people and listening with a heart. Driving back home, he let me explain everything that happened. When we were finally home, he let me know that I hadn't killed anyone. We learned that the teacher was taken from the hotel to a hospital. We knew he made it out of the emergency room and was in the hospital receiving critical care. The official story is that he was in a car accident but was going to live.

Once we learned what we needed to know about his condition and that I got lucky by not having killed him, I headed back to college. Dreams back on track. Like I said, keep moving.

Just to close the loop on that story... that teacher did not remain a teacher after this happened, and he did survive the injuries. All that is worth sharing is that my guidance counselor, Big G, is an Angel for a lot of reasons. I might add that he's an Angel to a lot of people I know and have learned about over the years.

As an adult ...

I'm not sure where you are in your journey. For me, taking on life as an adult was not easy. Mainly, because where I would cross the line into adulthood wasn't all that clear from where I was in high school.

In high school, I got into trouble in all the ways teenagers do. Drinking, smoking, chewing tobacco, skipping class, and teachers were beside themselves with me. But, growing up, I had also watched my brothers get involved in drugs, violence, jail, and prison. I also had a personal example of what it takes for a family to fall apart. I didn't want to make those choices in life. So, I did my best to do… something else. In my thinking, <u>anything else</u> was better so I just didn't copy my brothers. And I started thinking about other things like graduating high school and going to college.

What I learned is the more we know what superpowers we have, the easier it becomes to... persevere, manage our time in positive activity, stay motivated in what our dreams are, and after a while... we can appreciate the stability that comes from staying on course.

I might add…stability was a real nice experience I had never had until somewhere in the middle of high school. That stability came from Angels in high school

… and more than handful of others prior to that. I can't stress enough how important Angels are in this life.

Next ...

What's next?

Before we talk about what's next, I just want to thank you for letting me share my childhood story with you. I covered more than I'm comfortable sharing with anyone and more than I've ever shared with anyone in one setting. And I did it to hopefully encourage one of **three** things:

>> **If you are in the middle of some sort of hell,** my hope is that my sharing will encourage you to share your story with one trusted person. Look for that angel in your life and lean on them. That angel, your story, and seeing the other side are what you need right now. This is about empowerment, not falling into a victim mindset.

>> **If you have come out the other side** of some sort of hell you were in, my hope is that by me sharing, you will recognize that your story, too, is an inspiration. You have a unique experience that built in you something incredible to draw on for the strength you need to heal. And I hope you are on that path now.

>> **If you know someone** living in the thick of it, or trying to find a path away from it, then you know what makes these people, in your life, extraordinary.

Be willing to walk with them to a better place, show them another path, and be the angel they can lean on.

All three reasons as to why I shared my story are what it means to be **Resilient Now**.

So ... now, you ask: **What's Next?**

What's next is that we break the cycle of hell we came from. It's over. We are not letting the past be our future.

I mentioned it earlier in several places that just talking things through is valuable. It's a valuable part of healing. It's a valuable part of putting it behind us. It's a valuable part of shifting an attitude to something far more productive in life. And just by talking, we validate a lot of what makes us who we are. It also allows us to focus on all the strengths we've gathered and marshal all that goodness forward for us and others. It's healthy, and I am glad I could do that with you by writing the book. More importantly, I hope you found the journey worth the effort. My hope is that you can find just one person to share your story with. Share the good. Share the bad. Put it out there and work on what tomorrow looks like. That's healthy stuff.

I hope you're feeling inspired. Remember, resilience isn't just about enduring tough times; it's about rising stronger and wiser from them. That's where you and I are now. We aren't victims; we survive things, and we move on stronger and more able.

We are **Resilient Now**!

When you are ready to live life at your best, ask yourself some questions:

- How do you feel when you think about tomorrow? Do you like the way you feel?
- What one thing can you change today that makes later today or tomorrow better?
- Who is the one person you can talk to? Will you?
- Can you name one Angel in your life? How about two?
- Who needs to hear what's on your heart? Will you share it with them?
- How can you practice more self-compassion in your daily life? Is it something you will actually do?
- Are you actively seeking out opportunities for growth and learning?
- Who can you express gratitude to today? How will you do it?
- Do you need a helping hand? Will you be brave enough to ask?

In the next section of this book, I cover seven different mindsets that you can adopt today, and I share what my superpowers are.

I encourage you to read that section. And then ask yourself:

- Which mindset will you take on first?
- Which superpowers did you learn you have? Now, what are you going to do with it?

So, when you ask, what's next?

You now know the answer.

7 mindsets to be Resilient Now

> *Your character comes at a price. Be willing to pay that price.*
> *The goal is to be proud of what you paid for.*

There were seven of us in the house in the forest where this book started. There are two left today. Me and one of my big brothers. We are where we are because, well … we are Resilient Now.

But the truth of the matter is, for him, for me, for you, being resilient means that we are a work in progress. We aren't perfect. We aren't victims. We have tools. And we have Angels around us. The mindsets that I share in this part of the book are not something I could have shared when I was 18. I was just starting to learn about all these things back then. And as I write it today, I still have plenty that I work on every day, as you will read. I still fall down, and I still need people around me to help lift me back up. Angels have found me in my adult life as well, but that would be a whole new book. That may be the case for you, too.

So, this next section is just me sharing what I've learned growing up in all those stories I've shared, hoping that you can learn things earlier than I did. Hopefully, I help spark in you a revelation of what you have learned given your experiences. They may be similar– or you may think about it and find a whole new you waiting to just burst onto the scene and triumph over the hell that was your past. OR– maybe you know someone who has hardship in their past or is living in it now. If so, this may help you understand how they tick … what makes them extraordinary and how you can walk along with them to a better place.

The psychology behind and science that supports what Resilience is and how it is developed is complex, and there are tons of studies on it. If my studies on the topic had been done while in a PhD program, I would be called Dr. Dom today. – But as it is, here's what I have for you:

I've simplified all of it:

Resilience in 3 easy steps ☺, by Dom:

Resilience is a collection of real-world superpowers. And they are inside you, just waiting to either be <u>discovered</u>, <u>honed,</u> and/or <u>used</u>.

Successfully employing these superpowers looks like this:

1) **Realize you have the superpower.** Mine came from hardship during my young life. Some people develop a victim mindset after hardship. That's unfortunate, because that mindset only leads to a life rolling downhill. In my case, the superpower was planted when I was young– and I grew. I never saw myself as a victim.

2) **Hone those superpowers.** I honed them every time I had to lean on something to get past a hardship. In my case, I was doing so in survival mode, maybe not even aware of what superpowers were emerging at the time. I had plenty of hardship, but I also had Angels looking out for me (that I didn't realize until much later in life). As a result, I grew. Some people don't grow. Even worse is when the superpowers are never recognized in the first place, so they never actually help that person.

3) **Use them.** I did then, maybe without even knowing it, with the help of my Angels. I do use them now deliberately, with the help of my Angels and my family.

Think about elite-level achievements and who achieves them: Pro athletes, movie stars, television and stage actors and performers, business and industry titans, worldwide sensational musicians; all perform at elite levels in their field.

Every success you see at those levels employs three things in this order:

1. **They recognize their superpowers.**
2. **They hone those superpowers.**
3. **They use their superpowers.**

Then, they define a life outside and beyond where they started from. And they go about the process of achieving it.

Well – you and I can do that.

I might add, there is a tad bit of luck involved with their stories … as it is in the lives of my wife and me. But we defined our lives outside and beyond where we started from and went about achieving it. As a result:

- Our kids didn't move around as they grew up, like I had. They developed lifelong friends from kindergarten onward.
- My wife and I have been married over 33 years … and my model for what a marriage looks like was nothing like the one we are living.
- I had a successful 15-year career as an entrepreneur followed by an amazing 15 years as a senior executive in a Fortune 5 company, and that's rare for a guy like me who came from a

- broken home, on the street, and went to school for theatre.
- I am an accomplished advisor, entrepreneur, consultant, and author, and I flunked kindergarten to start the whole thing.
- We have a beautiful home and all the gardens we want to enjoy nature right out our front door. Hey– therapy is a good thing, and nature is a big one for us.

I've only shared those key achievements because in my mind, they are elite-level performance using the same tools as any other elite-level performer. To be even more clear– being rich has very little to do with money. And money has very little to do with how to measure what success looks like. As a result, I am rich. And those bullets above are my measures of success. And just because I list them as achievements, none were easy– and yours won't be either. They just take a mindset or two … or three, over time.

The reality is that experiences in life give each of us the opportunity to make choices about how we react to those experiences. What comes our way may not be in our control– but our reaction to them, what we learn because of them, and how we take lessons from them all help us build mindsets. Those mindsets can help us become a victim, OR those mindsets can help us recognize our superpowers. There really is only one good choice between the two.

How will you define what success looks like for you? Because now that you know the secret of elite performance… we have leveled the playing field.

I've already shared what success looks like to me. The way it looks in my adult life is that our kids didn't have the childhood I had. My wife and I didn't let my past become what they would have to live. I don't have the adult life my parents had. I chose a very different life on purpose. And our kids are starting their families where we all talk about love and life and goodness, celebrate birthdays, triumphs, and success. We ask for help, build our own traditions, laugh together, pray together, and we talk about the easy as well as the hard stuff of life.

This is what real success is … and I wish it for you. Not that I wish my life for you– I wish for you to have the life you deserve. And I know that takes work. More importantly, hopefully you see the key ingredients in you that feed your resilience to overcome, heal, thrive, and see the potential of your life. Resilience is what you are building in you so that you can succeed. And success today might be as simple as making sure you wake up tomorrow. And one day... it will be finding the path out of hell. Or maybe you have already done that, and now it's time to heal. This is worthy stuff. It's time to be **Resilient Now**.

Growing up, I learned I have superpowers, and I developed some key mindsets that are part of my adult life every day. If you are someone looking to find a path away from hell, or someone you love is, this part of the book is for you to tap into what being **Resilient Now** means.

My superpowers fall under one of these seven mindsets, and all of them came about during my younger life in school. I think they are, to some degree, anchors to where resilience finds footing for everyone:

- Listen to everything
- Provide value
- See through it
- Say, 'Yes, and …'
- Take responsibility
- Change
- Keep moving

Feel free to skip around and read what interests you. The key to this section is to help you uncover YOUR superpowers and know their value in your life.

Here they are one by one along with the superpowers that support each, at least for me:

Listen to everything

> **Watch your language ... it does stuff ... our goal should be that it does good and important stuff. Only.**

The seeds to these superpowers were planted even before I started school, when I was really young.

- **Expert Communication Skills.** You and I know what words mean and how to use them to get things done, to convey messages simply, to show understanding, and to teach and simplify. But sometimes we can use our words to cut like a razor's edge, can't we? Because that's true, we also must be careful how we use this skill.
  - This started for me back when I heard all the yelling in the house, the hard words, the silence of the forest, and how words from books built whole worlds. I was learning, then, what communication really is.

- **Empathy for others' situations.** Just because we have empathy, that doesn't mean we automatically jump in. It just means we understand where people are in their lives or in their troubles. And we understand it quicker than others might. We either jump in or watch everything to see what others do.
  - Growing up while we were still together, watching my brothers, their actions, their fears, and their

shenanigans: I took it all in and started to understand things even back then.

- **Emotional Intelligence (EI)**. This is what we use to maintain our ability to connect with others. This also means we have the EI to protect ourselves, which can be perceived as putting up walls that just can't be penetrated by anyone, no matter how close they are to us. You and I both know this is both true and sometimes necessary. But it's not always necessary, and we do it anyway. Because this is true, we have to keep ourselves in check. To be clear here, I'm still working on this one quite a bit with the people around me who I love.
- For me– this meant I grew up a little faster than most, learning, seeing, and being part of more adult situations way too early. This also meant I had to learn how to deal with things a little sooner and differently than most.

- **Ability to be self-reliant.** Generally, this is a good thing since we can take care of ourselves without much bother. But it also means we don't ask for help when we could or even should. We might be a 'loner' too—for no good reason—or perceived as one—for good reason. So, finding a way to balance that is something we have to work on, where others seem to get it much easier.
- Unfortunately, that began back when I would find myself alone in the forest. But it also meant I learned how to take care of myself way too early—and it stuck as a real-life skill.

Provide value

> **Hopefully you will have to go way beyond yourself to serve someone else. Hopefully.**

My whole career has revolved around **providing value**, the kind that makes someone else's job or life easier. This is what my grampa showed me. It's what all the Angels in my life did for me. It's what I know … and so it's how I try to live.

But if you are like me, providing value for people has two sides in our adult life:

On the one hand, we know when someone has offered something special to us. At the time, I wasn't aware, but looking back as an adult, neglect during my young life had a way of teaching that to me. Maybe that's the case in your life or in someone you know. In my case, it was people offering food, or clothing, or a job, or a place to be… safe… with no strings attached… as a gift. It's a kind of appreciation we have that many may not, and we have no idea how to ask for it in the first place, so we don't. We become overwhelmed when it's given, however. And yes, that follows us into adult life, married life, parenthood, and our careers.

On the other hand, since we know just how powerful it is to receive that kind of gift, we can see when giving that sort of gift will be that powerful for someone else. We know the value of the smallest act of kindness that we can offer anyone. We can see the pressure that others are under and where we can fill a gap that can stop the pressure from crushing them. Somehow, we know in our hearts if that gap can be filled with a sincere smile, letting them know that we see them, or if we need to lend a hand or jump in with them to carry the load for them. We can see problems before they are problems and find the way around them—and people may never know we did something to help save them from the issue. We know how to give—even if people don't see it. We know they will feel it. And we don't care who gets the credit.

For me, as I look at my career, I recognize that other people in business do things with greater ease than me. Others might have better training than me or experience to get things done a certain way in life, in business, or in their personal matters. They may have had a much different upbringing or different schooling aligned to their career, or they may just be smarter than I am when it comes to the task at hand, whatever that may be.

I'm OK with all of that. Rarely is competing with anyone what motivates me. I also know that many people just don't try to achieve things in life because they don't know how to make it easy. I know people don't try because they don't have the training or experience. Or they don't try because they can see that failure might be an option, and they lose interest. So, if there are similarities for you along these lines, then we have a leg up on those people. We can do things that aren't easy. And we can figure things out without the training that school might have given us. We don't know that something can't be done, and so we do. And I bet you look for others who you can help along the way, don't you? This is how we provide value.

Once elementary school started, these seeds were planted and grew over time:

- **Problem solving.** Of course, this has two sides to it. I tend to think everything is a problem that can be solved. I drive my family crazy because I am constantly asking when I walk into the room, 'What's the problem?' or 'How goes it?' as if there is something wrong and I'm there to fix it. Usually, they are all just fine, and they ignore me... in a loving way. Does this happen with you too? The other side of this is that if there is a problem, we are generally ready, willing, and able, and people know they can count on us to help.

- **Creativity.** I have some creative outlets. How about you? Drawing, painting, woodworking, gardening. I even went to college for degrees in Theatre, Design and Directing. Both personally and professionally, I like to see great pictures emerge, good people doing great things, and then see the magic of life unfold everywhere. You see what I mean? Even that was just a little too dramatic!

- **Collaboration.** This one is a bit tricky for me. On the one hand, I like to 'go it alone' and can handle things on my own, quite well, I think. But on the other hand, there is nothing more invigorating than a solid topic to discuss with passionate people to land on some like-minded conclusions or decisions or an expanded understanding to move things forward. The debates can be strong but always respectful. The work is rewarding, even if it's exhausting. But when it comes to small talk… eh… I can walk away from that, no problem, even less interest. Sometimes people misinterpret my actions along these lines. Anything similar for you along these lines?

- **Independence.** Elementary school is probably the place where resilience manifested itself first, for me. If that's the case with you too, then you know that when no one is giving us guidance or telling us what to do next, we make all the decisions. We find a way to motivate ourselves to do the next thing. We don't see ourselves as a victim; we are either surviving or we just consider the life we have to be normal, and we know what needs to be done next. Sometimes, however, the next step should be to ask for some help. You and I sometimes skip that step, don't we?

See through it

> "
> **Having 'Hope' doesn't mean everything is easy and fine… It simply means working on something and believing in it because it is good.**
> "

Things come to an end. Good things and bad both come to an end. So …

'Start with the end in mind.' It's a pretty common approach in business, so teams can design a path to get there. And leaders use it to ask all the questions about their company and people to determine the risk and how to mitigate it along those paths. It's almost the same thing as 'seeing through it'. It's how we see the end and keep it in mind.

Obviously, I love this concept. Both professionally and personally, you and I automatically use this kind of thinking to set guardrails in our lives. In my case, when my wife and I decided to have kids, I said that I wanted our kids to have a one-school-district life. A place where they can develop lifelong friendships and grow up without having to move from school to school. Thankfully, the one-school-district life was the experience my wife had growing up, and we agreed on it for our family. That was us putting the end in mind and establishing the guardrails. As we raised our kids, we lived in three homes across that time. All those homes were in the same school district; we just needed more space as the family grew. And all three kids grew up attending the same elementary, middle, and high schools in one school district. Today, they and we have lifelong friendships and a family home we call the safe house. That was another thing we wanted to make sure we provided. A home... a place to be. Something stable and always there, with food... and family dinner time and Thanksgiving traditions.

You and I have been through plenty. Let's look at the tough stuff: We were there before it came into our lives. We lived through it. On the other side, we can take stock of the bruises and cuts and look at things afterwards. Because it was intense for us—it's probably more vivid in our minds than what others may remember about their life experiences. That's OK.

It's OK because we use that. We see through the hell we were in and what the other side looks like. And we do what it takes to get there. Now, saying this isn't easy at all. It's not simple. I have one brother who didn't make it through the mess in front of him and he took his own life. Another had other mental health issues along with drug abuse that finally got the best of him as well. And my oldest brother drank himself to the point where he couldn't see the next day. And he didn't make it either. We live on beyond these things. They hurt. They are real. We are still here, and we must carry on.

> ***Side note:*** I am going to pause for a really important thought here.
>
> We CAN make it through it. Now, if you need help with any mental health concerns, just ask anyone for the help. There isn't a soul around you who won't get you to the person you need to sit with next. If you are the one that can't see what tomorrow looks like because you are overwhelmed or drugs or alcohol make it a little cloudy, tell anyone around you. Call a random number from your phone, and the person who answers will help... NO ONE wants to see anyone blinded to what their potential is. You are that important, and you are worth it. People like my mom, dad, and brothers never reached out. And I was just lucky enough to have Angels get in my way, blocking the path to hell. I'm lucky to have had such people– I encourage you to just let someone know. I've included resources at the back of the book if you or someone you love needs them.

I encourage you to see through whatever or wherever you are right now. That is how resilience, which lives inside you, is unleashed: By someone else close to you. Let them in to do it. Even today, I still must remind myself to let people in who are closest to me and care. It's not easy: I get it. I know where you are. Let's win today.

To simplify this, I think of hard times having three parts to them:

> -The beginning.

> -The part we live through.

> -And the other side.

That middle part requires some superpowers, here are mine:

- **Critical Thinking.** There are about a zillion aptitude, management, professional, and psychological type tests where 'Critical Thinking' is one of the things measured. I always tested high, fell strongly in that quadrant, or had it as one of my top three things they measured. That's all well and good, but my guess is neither you nor I need any tests to tell us where we land on all the charts.

  If critical thinking is high for you, then you know we can take in tons of information and consider all of it very quickly, seeing patterns, groupings, and connections quicker than others might. Some may say we are overly pragmatic (well, I've made a career out of that), meaning we may lack emotion. But the truth is that when nobody is looking, we cry too, and earlier than most watching emotional movies, for instance, because we see what's coming before others do. We just don't cry when there is something that needs to get done. We figure it out.

- **Adaptability.** Believe it or not, not everyone has this skill or attribute at all. In fact, I get frustrated when others seem to lose their cool when things go from calm to chaos. If this is true for you, we know that we can behave just fine in either calm or chaos, and the transition doesn't mess us up at all either. Some see it as us not caring. But again, the truth is we care a great deal and are trying to figure out how to get everyone else comfortable in the new environment because we are already there.

- **Patience.** This is another tricky one. People never use the word 'patient' to describe me. If people say that about you too, you know it's our personal hidden gem and maybe our definition is different than what most people think. We can endure longer than anyone else in any situation.

At a young age for me, it meant I could go a day with no prospect of eating, for instance– or a week without a plan on where I might sleep. A month ahead of me and no idea who will still be around me next month. Or a long year of shifting from one place to another to another and yet another.

If you are like me, we have two modes: we wait, or we act. We see others break, and we never have. We won't. We don't break.

Say, 'Yes, and …'

> **Real discovery happens in your mind… and the most profound discoveries are found in your heart.**

I read an article once by a prominent businessperson who suggested that if any of us are ever offered an incredible job or opportunity that we are not skilled enough to accept, accept it. And then learn what you need to learn, fast.

In college, I was a theatre major. Design and Directing were my focus. There is an improvisation activity where actors take turns building a story. The first actor says something and asks a question of the second. The second actor must answer, 'Yes, and...' then build on the story that leads to a handoff to the third actor, who also must say, 'Yes, and...' continuing to build on it from there. So, on and so on for all the actors playing. The story builds and builds and becomes ever more entertaining, enjoyable, and fun.

Once someone says 'no'... that story is over. There is no more reason to talk about it. It can't be built on. It's done. I never forgot the first time I played it in school. I had been doing it my whole life; it seemed... taking where I was and building on it from there.

Think of what we've heard in our lives. We know what 'no' sounds like better than most. We know how ideas and dreams we've had never even gotten off the ground, either because we heard 'no' or we heard nothing at all, or because we had to focus on surviving, so we never asked.

The best parts of my learning have always been when I heard someone encourage an idea by saying 'yes, and...' then build on it from there, joining me and making it our story from then on. In no time, it's joint ownership; it's a better idea than the one that started the conversation, and what happens next is of interest to both people building the story.

As you and I move on in life, we know how important it is when someone tells us their thoughts. We know that saying "yes ... I like those thoughts, and I'd like to build on them with you." Is the most important thing that person may hear, especially if they are young. If we are approaching work or your career this way, I can tell you that is the fastest way to have a company, a team, or project move forward. When someone says, 'yes, and...' instead of 'no, because ...', or flat-out 'no', things are awesome.

There are a couple quotes I love that come from the Stoics and the philosophy of life they documented. The first is from Epictetus: *"Do not seek for things to happen the way you want them to; rather, welcome things that happen in whichever way they happen."* And the next is from

Marcus Aurelius' timeless wisdom: *"A blazing fire makes flame and brightness out of everything that is thrown into it."*

Both quotes capture a mindset that can be summed up in one simple phrase: '**Amore Fati.**'

A fun story here is that my youngest daughter has those words: 'Amor Fati' tattooed on her arm. But the font she chose is a little hard for me to read, so, to me, it looks like it says, "Acorn Baby." So, when we agree on something after arguing, I finish the conversation with "Acorn Baby!" Fun stuff.

So, if you were to ask, "Hey Dom... If you had to give one piece of advice for people to be happy, what would it be?"

I think back to Mr. H in 5th grade who planted some mighty seeds of resilience in me. As an adult, they have grown into an answer to that question about what it takes to be happy.

I would have to say that when you are engaging with others, say, 'Yes, and...' then add something wonderful to it. Encourage their thoughts to bloom. It makes for the best conversations.

You and I both know that idea stems from simply accepting the way things are... and… going on from there.

I have found in life that the surest way for people to be sad is for them to experience life around them but not enjoy it because it's not the way they wanted it to be, or it isn't as they had envisioned it in their head. Somehow, they expect life to be a certain way and are beside themselves when it isn't that way. So, they are miserable because the way they want to see it in their head never happens. As a result, they miss what did happen and can't see that it is probably just as good as what they expected, maybe even better. What a disappointment.

Mr. H planted the skills to watch things unfold, take them in, and then move things forward in a positive, enjoyable way, whatever the situation might be, are:

- **Flexibility**. There are two kinds of people. Those who are not flexible are one kind of person. We know who these people are. We all know someone like this. And the other kind of people are the flexible type. When people are busy fretting or worrying about anything—where to eat, what color to go with, or where to go next—they seldom worry about the flexible people in their lives. They happen to know that the flexible people will be good with anything they land on. The flexible people will love whatever choice they make.

    I'm the flexible type. If you are too, then we both know that sometimes people think we just don't care. Well, we know that's not the case, but it's too hard to explain to people sometimes. I say, 'Stay flexible.' It's a better place to be because we actually do love it either way, and that makes for a much better life. Enjoy being flexible and maybe even a little misunderstood, even if those around you don't understand it.

- **Risk-taking**. If you are like me, we've learned some incredible ways to minimize risk in our lives. Heck, we walked around cliffs our whole childhood, so we have developed some extra ways to climb rocks and avoid falling that others just don't have. So, when it comes to taking a risk, to us, that just means that we go about minimizing all the potential ways to fall so we can take our steps across the cliff wall.

We do that, while others simply won't try because the risk is too great.

- **Resourcefulness**. I roll with the punches. What about you? If so, we just go find the things we need to do, whatever it is that needs done next, right? We don't think of limitations first. We think of the necessary steps and what it will take to achieve each step. That might mean we have to go get some things along the way, but that's never stopped us in the past. We don't see any of that as a limitation.

When you grew up with nothing, starting with nothing isn't scary.

Take responsibility

> "
> **Decide which words you will live by to change the world...
> ~Appreciation, Forgiveness, Love, Gratitude, Honesty… (These are some good ones.)**
> "

There are plenty of hard experiences in my life, but you have tough experiences too. I've been hurt, and people often ask me how I go about forgiving people who have hurt me. People have asked if I have forgiven my mom, for instance, or my dad. Generally, I don't answer people that ask me about it unless I can help them with something they are trying to figure out regarding offering forgiveness in their life.

What I will share with you is that I think there are plenty of characters in my stories to consider. I'm only telling my side of this story. There is my mom. There are my four brothers. There is my dad. All these people, along with me, have had to deal with more than a few hardships. All of us were ill-equipped for the things going on in our lives, and none of us were seeking or getting desperately needed help. There are plenty of people, events, stories, or parts of stories to relate to, and there is no shortage of the need for forgiveness all the way around. All the lives in my family have been filled with drugs / alcohol / violence / neglect / financial hardship... the list goes on, and we never talked about any of it.

Looking back now, sure, I wish that we had been the kind of family that could talk about the problems going on. And, looking back, I wish we would have recognized the need for help in lots of ways. But when we were in the thick of things—as I've already shared—it seemed normal. People who have never been there can't understand it because it seems so different from their lives. And people looking from the outside can condemn all kinds of things and think they know who hurt who, who needs to forgive who, and who is responsible for this or that.

If that's going on in your life, ignore them all. You are in the thick of it, or you know what the thick of it meant to you now that you've grown and are living life beyond it. I shared a quote at the beginning of this chapter that I wrote years ago because, at some point, we all do need to pick some words that are going to be our guardrails.

"
**Decide which words you will live by to change the world...
~Appreciation, Forgiveness, Love, Gratitude, Honesty… (These are some good ones.)**
"

Let's use what we have learned to pick the right words as we take responsibility for our lives from here forward. None of us needs more people looking into our lives and telling us the things that are wrong. What the world needs more of is people caring enough to walk with us in the thick of it by joining us, not telling us what they see wrong or who isn't doing what they should be doing. Just join in and help lead us to a better path or walk with us to a better place.

So, when asked about forgiveness, I like to ask in return: Who do you think begins to heal when you offer forgiveness? This is the idea I am reminded of when there is forgiveness to be given.

There is another side to what it means to take responsibility:

Most people associate the idea of taking responsibility and apply it when something that has gone wrong or needs to be fixed. Looking at the stories I've shared, I've seen plenty of very poor decisions (mine and decisions of those around me) play out in my life, watching my family crumble. Decisions have consequences and impact others. This is true. But, I can't take responsibility for others. I can only take responsibility for myself– and this is what that looks like to me:

Taking responsibility means grabbing the reins when life gets wild. It means breaking down my dreams into bite-sized pieces and tackling them one bite at a time.

I must do this. You must do this. We've got this.

Back to that first definition, accepting blame is certainly not the most important definition of responsibility to me; I hope it's not for you either. It's important, but there's so much more to it. If you are like me, we use our skills to take responsibility, not run from it. We own things to make things better for others and ourselves. We own them early, and we aren't thinking of the liability most people think of when we take on the responsibility of something.

Watching and learning how my family fell apart, the violence it takes for that to happen (big and small) all point to the seedlings of critical skills that I have honed as an adult to take responsibility for what I can control in my own life.

Depending on where you are in your journey to overcome hardship, you may be in the process of developing these superpowers as well:

- **Accountability:** This just means we take ownership of our actions and the consequences. It also means we don't shy away from admitting mistakes or failures. In fact, we are the ones who keep working to make things right. People recognize this about us and know we can be relied upon to follow through on commitments. We set clear expectations, meet deadlines, and don't make excuses when things get tough.

We also recognize people who may perceive accountability only as a form of blame or fault-finding. Look– I've learned to just disregard those people who constantly point fingers or hold others to impossibly high standards without taking responsibility for their own actions. Ironically, these tend to be the people who blame others for not taking responsibility for how our actions make them feel. They might be right. We don't hold ourselves accountable for how others feel about us; that's their business.

- **Decision-making.** If you are like me, we make choices with confidence and clarity, and usually much quicker than other people. We aren't afraid to weigh the options, consider the consequences, and take decisive action, even in the face of uncertainty. Sometimes we get it right. Sometimes we get it wrong, but then we can also make quick decisions to set things right.

  We do our best to seek input from others if we can, but something most people miss about us is that if we don't have the time to seek input from others, we do our best to consider what their input would be to help us shape our decision. If time allows, we find out if our guess was right by asking them. If things are moving fast, we trust we got it pretty close and make the decision. You and I have been accused of being impulsive– right? But we know we are being thoughtful and strategic in our decision-making process, aiming for the best possible outcome for all involved given the timeline we have.

This is a quality leadership trait or skill. You and I just must live with the fact that we won't please everyone with our decisions all the time.

- **Leadership.** First, anyone, including you and me, who influences anyone to do anything, good or bad, is a leader. The idea of leadership has nothing to do with a title we hold. Our life experiences have put us in a place where our actions and our words influence other's actions and words. Hopefully, we make conscious decisions to inspire and motivate others to achieve great goals. Some ingredients that play a major role in positive leadership are leading by example, having integrity and empathy, and empowering those around us to reach their full potential.

  Our particular brand of leadership includes adding other perspectives to what we see and fostering a culture of collaboration and innovation. We love to see and encourage creativity; embrace differing thoughts to see just how big and how far an idea, team, group, or project can go.

  But... we also get excited to move fast and can sometimes be perceived as authoritarian or dictatorial, or maybe we even dominate conversations and, in so doing, miss input from others. Now that we both know this, we have something to work on and keep in check. Hopefully, we also have a friend who can put their hand on our shoulder to help us slow down. I have several. I call all of them Angels.

- **Self-discipline** is a hard skill for others to attribute to us. Maybe it's another hidden gem we lean on when we need to, and others just can't see it. You and I do set goals, and we do achieve them. We just may not do either one in a traditional way. That's because to achieve anything in our lives, we have had to constantly adjust things to deal with obstacles. This means we didn't set out with a known plan and milestones... and then tell the world. Maybe we told no one because there was no one to tell.

So, although people may not use the phrase, 'self-discipline' to describe you or me, the way we may use it to describe a soldier, they might have a curiosity about our ability to maintain focus and persevere even in the harshest of circumstances, or deal with unbelievable distractions and yet still perform. Maybe they will simply recognize our sense of commitment to someone or something and our ability to manage our time effectively but not know how to think about it. We know what the superpower really is. We have had to rely on it to get where we are today.

Change

> **The future: Don't fret over the future. You are in the process of building it, so... carry on and get it right.**

I'm totally comfortable with things changing around me. Well, that's not entirely true. I don't like the way prices of things keep going up and up and up, especially at the grocery store. I'm a sometimes chef and artisan bread master… I digress.

Change was a constant in my life. Changes in schools; homes; places where I slept; food that I ate & when I ate it; places where I worked; people that helped me along the way; the families who took an interest in me. All of it represents plenty of change in my life.

How about you?

We all know that saying: The only thing that never changes is that life is always changing. Or something like that. We've all heard version of the saying.

There is a whole science behind something called 'Change Management'. There are graphs showing the various stages and the types of feelings that people experience in each phase. It's a giant industry that covers every industry revolving around the human condition. The whole idea is rooted in the fact that people don't like to change, and yet, all of us must change over time. Jobs, people, environments—everything changes. Sometimes the change is abrupt, and sometimes it happens over longer periods of time.

But if you've dealt with trauma and change as a constant growing up, we have something in common. We have dealt with change like a speed dating night. Everything changed for us all the time, so the phases all blur together for us because they just happen so quickly. We've mastered it!

Here's a pretty famous graphic showing what those stages of change look like for most people and organizations:

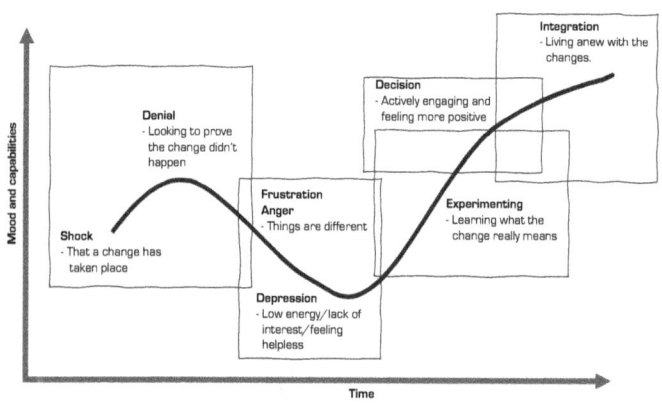

So, we don't go through the normal feelings of

shock or denial. We don't get frustrated or fall into depression. We actually embrace and weave in and out of experimenting, making decisions and integrating things into our life, quickly, so we don't get tripped up. Other people sometimes break before they can make it through all the phases of change. We don't break; and sometimes we have to lead the effort. In my professional life, change management is something I am called on to help teams and companies manage through. So, yes, these mindsets are real, and the skills we have developed all help us overcome hardship even in adulthood.

By 7th grade, and as I entered junior high, these superpowers were starting to grow:

- **Innovation**. It's part of our problem-solving skill set. You and I try to improve on everything, including the things we've done in the past. We just believe that there is a better way, and we go about finding it. I can't tell you how many times I have made the best pesto… yet. And it's always getting better, plus I learn some things I shouldn't do in any future attempt. I haven't even written down the recipe after 10 years of trying things because I know I can make it better next time.

- **Learning**. Everything we do is a learning experience. I don't think I have any other kind of experience. If that's you too, we use what we learn doing anything in order to help us make doing what we do next even better. That's our goal, anyway. That's our mindset. In fact, this mindset allows us to break cycles that have been destructive in the past. It allows us to move past something by going around it instead of through it, or vice versa. Or it makes going through something if we must, as a survivor instead of a victim at some level.

- **Growth**. A growth mindset is the most rewarding mindset to have professionally. It allows us to know just how far we could go and keeps us fully aware of where we want to go next. It's the best of both worlds. I know plenty of people who just plod along only to find that they are miserable since they aren't growing. With a growth mindset, we are always resetting what growth looks like from where we are, so, enjoyment in the journey is real for us.

Keep moving

> **There are two kinds of mountains:
> those you climb when you must,
> and those you must climb.**

The idea to 'Keep Moving' hinges on a few skills that develop with life experiences. My experiences and the stories I've shared from high school are where each of these superpowers were either planted, were identified or where I started to hone them:

- **Perseverance.** You and I know what it's like to have to do it over and over because it isn't quite working out. Go the extra distance we never saw when we started down the road. Deal with an environment we weren't prepared for when we started a task. We have seen others fall by the wayside, and we didn't, mainly because we couldn't. We had no other option. This is where we developed this superpower.

- **Time Management.** We never called it that until someone told us that was what it was. In the thick of things, we just had to get done with one thing to get to the next. We didn't have an option. So, we paced ourselves to do it in the time we gave ourselves. And we do it with some expertise today. In fact, one whole piece of coaching I offer professionals is on 'time-blocking' so they can put their day in order, making sure everything they committed to is accomplished, and then some.

- **Self-Motivation.** We never called it that growing up, either. We simply don't need people or others to tell us what the next thing is. We can see it, and we can see its value, so we go about getting it done.

- **Appreciation for stability.** When things are working, the way they should, we have a supreme appreciation watching and observing it all happen. We know, better than most, what it takes for anything to be stable. And we understand the value because, better than most, we know how to compare it to the chaos that could be instead. Some people just like it to be stable and lose it when it's not. That's not us.

I shared a big list of superpowers here!

I'm sharing about all these skills and abilities, or superpowers, traits … whatever you want to call them because we all need to be reminded what superpowers we have or are developing so we never live our life as victims.

And... if you are living life with a victim mindset, you need to be talked out of it. That's no way to live life.

The fact is, you and I have had tremendous experiences that have taught us more than a few things in some unique ways. I say we use them to go do great things!

Feel free to list your own superpowers… you probably have others or more! This list just happens to be mine, meant to create a spark for you to identify yours.

Which mindset will you start the day with tomorrow so you can be **Resilient Now**?

Some final thoughts:

The resilience that we rely on needs to be fed with goodness. Here are a few nuggets to help strengthen those skills, attributes, and traits we already have in us. Hopefully you can find something here and make it your own:

- **Faith.** If you have faith in something higher, something bigger than yourself– then nurture it. If that means prayer, then find time to pray. If that means meditation, find time to meditate. If that means learning from a holy book or scripture, find the time to study.

    > ***Side note:*** - Faith plays a significant role in my life. I didn't include it as a main chapter for two reasons. People have a strong reaction to the idea of religion and would simply dismiss this book as a religious book had I led with it. The second reason is that I think religion has very little to do with faith. I do think that Faith has plenty to do with God. And I believe God is personal– meaning, it's between you and God. Religion is simply how groups of people gather around a set of interpretations they all want to talk about - but that part is rarely the personal connection with God.

Personally, I believe that the most powerful forces on earth are Prayer, Forgiveness and Gratitude. And each point to something much greater than me - to something I believe God has given us. I embrace my faith. I encourage you to make it personal too, setting religion aside for this part of your journey.

- **Get Connected:** Building strong, healthy relationships with loved ones and friends can provide essential support during both good and bad times. Consider volunteering or joining a faith or spiritual group to connect with others.

For me– we are involved with several charities, and volunteer (not) regularly (enough). And we have faith communities we lean into, as well as healthy hobbies and lifelong friends that we meet with often.

- **Find Meaning Every Day:** Engage in activities that give you a sense of success and purpose. Set clear goals that you can achieve, helping you look toward the future with meaning.

For me– I block time, both personally and professionally, dedicated to working on both short- and long-term goals. I try to build something into my life every day. I've even developed little templates to keep myself organized.

- **Learn from the Past:** Reflect on how you've coped with past troubles. Identify patterns in your behavior and use these insights to guide your actions in the future. Consider keeping a journal to track your experiences.

For me— I'm not a huge journal guy like one of my daughters, but I am a note-taker and paper list maker. This book was one way for me to pull my notes all into one place to, in fact, document what I've learned from the past— so far.

- **Stay Hopeful:** While you can't change the past, you can always look toward the future. Being open to change makes it easier to adapt and view new challenges with less worry.

For me— The one sure thing I know in life is that I own and control my attitude. It's my choice how I react and where I allow my mind to dwell.

- **Take Care of Yourself:** Prioritize self-care. Engage in activities and hobbies you enjoy, include physical activity in your routine, get enough sleep, and maintain a healthy diet. Practice stress management techniques like yoga, meditation, or deep breathing.

For me— I do it all, and I still have stress to manage, so I have things to work on. Not everything on this list is easy, and I didn't say it was an easy list. Life takes work. Enjoy the work!

- **Take Action:** Rather than feeling stuck, take proactive steps to address challenges. Seek professional help when needed, and don't hesitate to reach out to others for support.

  For me– Sometimes I act too quickly. What I'm working on is slowing down and including more people in my processes. I've found things only get better, even if they take more time. I'm learning to be OK with that.

And finally: Remember that resilience won't eliminate life's problems, but it can help you navigate them more effectively and find joy even during difficult times.

About:

> **Setting aside time to be grateful changes everything. Everything.**

About the book:

After I finished writing the very first draft of this book, I reread it to see what themes I had captured, if any. I think there are two. The first theme is that all of us are made up of incredible stories. The story of anyone, on the surface, that they tell us in 30 seconds, or that we make up simply by meeting someone, is never the real story. I shared mine along the way early in the book. The things we share might cover some facts–but usually not the stuff of life that makes us human and beautiful. Theme one is that learning what makes people human and beautiful is worth the effort. In fact, it's the real stuff of life, and it's what real Angels do in this life.

Theme two is that success, as I've come to realize, looks very different from being famous, or having the top job, driving the fanciest cars, or living in the biggest house on the block. Instagram may tell us something different… but don't believe it.

Real success looks like making it through the challenges we're facing right now, waking up with determination not to be beaten, and surpassing our own bar every day. So, I say, believe this about yourself: You are the 'One in a million' – there just may not be a million followers giving you a 'thumbs up.'

I'm fortunate in that I've had several different things in my adult life fall into place. Positive things, awesome things like marriage, having children, great jobs, and various successes. All of them together are much bigger than my dreams as a kid. People who knew parts of my childhood would ask, "How did you do that?" or "How did you overcome that?" or "How did you beat those odds?"

I never liked those questions, and I always had a short answer to stop the conversation. But people who know me have always told me that my stories would be helpful to someone. I didn't understand what they meant. How could my stories be helpful?

So, I never intended to write this book. I hesitated for two reasons.

The first is that I didn't want to put my life out there as some sort of spectacle for people to say 'oooh' and 'ahhhhh' as they read these things. It's not useful to anyone to encourage people to feel pity or to feel sorry for me or my family.

The second reason I hesitated to write this book is because it's in my nature to help people. I didn't want to write a book full of these stories if it wasn't going to help someone. But I know that hardship can teach things. Personally, I've learned a lot. And if the two of us, me and you (as the reader of this book), can learn how valuable what we've learned really is, then I'm willing to join in.

So - I did write the book. Ultimately, my sharing these stories is about creating a space for you to reflect on your own journey. Maybe you will nod along, thinking, "Yeah, I've been there too." Or perhaps you will be reminded of moments when you thought you couldn't go on, but somehow you did. And I would say, that's powerful. If you happen to be a younger reader, something in these stories might resemble something going on in your life right now. Just know that I do understand. Together, we will learn some important things about our lives. The goal then is to get to the other side. This book, your angels, your superpowers, and your decision to be Resilient Now are all tools in our toolbox. Use them.

About resilience:

Resilience is a concept that my wife introduced to me. One evening we were talking about the blessings in our lives. At the time, those blessings included three children that we had raised and kept promises to. Our kids were all on their own, and we were new empty nesters. We both had fulfilling careers, and there was a real opportunity for both of us to retire early from our professional lives and pursue other dreams. Most of our marriage, to that point, included enough food for everyone and a home where friends and family all felt welcome. You could say we were counting our blessings.

The topic of **resilience** surfaced as I reflected on how I had dealt with certain challenges. Among other loved ones, as an adult, I've lost three brothers, two parents, and a Grampa who was more than a father figure to me. I've had (giant) ups and (big) downs professionally, and personally. My wife knows all about my upbringing and what I've been through during childhood. My wife, always supportive, lovingly remarked that my resilience would enable me to tackle whatever else life threw my way. She's been a big champion since we married. Even during rough patches in our marriage or my career, she stood as a champion for me to never have my past follow me into the future.

Years before that night, she was the first to suggest that I consider sharing my experiences to assist others in overcoming their own hardships. This conversation took place amidst the chaos of raising our children and juggling work to make ends meet. It's possible we were even navigating a rough patch in our marriage at the time. Her insight was that by opening up, I could potentially inspire others to tap into their resilience, whether they were young people or facing challenges later in life as adults.

That was the first time I let that suggestion go in one ear and out the other. I thought no one could benefit from my losing family members as one example—lots of people lose loved ones during their lives. My wife was just talking crazy talk, I thought. But the reality is that she saw a big picture while I was still in survival mode, a sort of tunnel vision, looking at one thing all by itself.

For a quick point of reference:

Resilience refers to the ability to recover and rebound from challenges and setbacks. It's a mental reservoir of strength that helps individuals handle stress and adversity as it comes up in life. I looked it up years ago when she brought it up so that I understood what she was talking about. There's actually a test to help educators measure this with students who have had childhood trauma and hardship. Yes … I took the test. You know– for fun.

But what we all know is that resilience is not a fixed asset like the color of our eyes. It can be developed and strengthened over time, and the things that make us resilient can change over time. In most people, the seeds of resilience are sown in our early experiences in life. And the more we rely on those tools, the stronger they become until, well, they become a superpower that we learn how to leverage in life.

I believe those superpowers start as little seeds planted when we are young. With each situation, hardship, or trauma in life, various skills, mindsets and strengths grow from those seeds. And then we rely on those tools and hone them.

As you have learned, the topic here for this entire book is Resilience. The question now is: What will your next step be? If you want advice from me: Be Resilient Now.

BONUS CONTENT

I often work with people in one-on-one conversations, professionally. For whatever reason, I've been blessed with the ability to create a space where people open their hearts and share their struggles, pressures, hardships, and triumphs. Sometimes, these conversations turn into meaningful discussions about hope and learning.

Over time, I've captured some of the topics that have made a difference in their lives—or mine from real conversations. And in most cases, my contributions are all the result of all the stories I've shared with you in this book.

If you're seeking a boost in some area of your life to help navigate hardships you've endured (or are currently facing), know this: simply recognizing that need already shows your strength—more than many realize. Keep going!

My hope is that you find something here that helps. These are all summaries of things that come up in conversations I have with people when we talk about their journey in life.

- Reframe Negative Thoughts: We need to look at negative situations realistically, but in a way that doesn't center on blame or brooding over what cannot be changed. Instead of viewing adversity as insurmountable, we need to reframe our thoughts to look for small ways to tackle the problem and make changes that will help.

Focusing on the positive things we can do is a great way to get out of a negative mindset. This approach can also help us better cope with challenges long-term. Think about challenges in more positive, hopeful ways. This way, instead of getting stuck in a loop of negative emotions, we learn to see these events as opportunities to challenge ourselves, develop new skills and grow.

- **Seek Support:** It took me a lifetime to finally look back and see all the Angels in my life that I could have leaned on but didn't. They had to muscle their way into my life, and I'm so grateful they did! And I'm not saying that just talking about life's difficulties makes them go away. I am saying that I have learned that sharing with a supportive friend or loved one makes me feel like I have someone in my corner. Support alone helps us develop stronger resilience in life. As a bonus, discussing things with others can also help us gain insight on the challenges we are facing or even come up with new ideas for managing them. Give it a try.

- **Focus On What Is Within Control:** When faced with a crisis or problem, it can be easy to get overwhelmed by things that feel far beyond our control. Instead of wishing there was some way to go back in time or change things, it can be helpful to try focusing on what we can directly impact. The things we own, like decisions we make in response to things that come our way.

Even when the situation seems dire, taking realistic steps can help improve it. No matter how small these steps may be, they can improve your sense of control and resilience.

To give you a visual, think of a round target or dartboard. Those things that fall inside the bullseye are what we can control. Those things that fall into the next ring out are things we might be able to influence or interact with directly, but we don't control that stuff. The third ring out and beyond are out of our control. All those things are there, and we must deal with them, but that's all we have. Know what's in your bullseye and what isn't.

- **Manage Stress:** I have a weakness here that I'm working on. Building healthy stress management habits is an effective way to increase overall resilience. These habits could include behaviors that help overall health, like getting enough sleep and exercise, as well as specific actions to take during moments of stress, like:

- Various breathing exercises. My middle daughter sparked this interest in me as she became a Certified Yoga instructor.
- Expressive writing. I encourage this for anyone, writer or not. I have hundreds of writing prompts that I have developed to help disrupt my thinking as well as clients and friends and family.
- Muscle relaxation. This is a real weakness of mine, and I would benefit tremendously if I could master this. I carry stress in my neck, and it's a mess. I actually have to work with a surgical neck specialist from time to time to ward off eventual surgery. So, this is real. Hopefully, you can master it quickly!

- **Keep in mind...** When you're stressed, it can be all too easy to neglect your own needs. Losing your appetite, ignoring exercise, and not getting enough sleep are all common reactions to a crisis situation. Instead, focus on building your self-nurturing skills, even when you're troubled. Make time for activities that you enjoy. This is probably why I have no shortage of hobbies. I have teased my wife that my hobbies are cheaper than therapy– but that's probably not true anymore, looking at all the activities I do that I enjoy and that I spend money on.

- **Believe in Your Abilities:** I think the older I get, the more I have a problem with this one. Professionally, I have been surrounded by some brilliant people. It has been hard for me to know where and how I fit in offering what I have to give compared to how impressive they are. But as a youngster, I never once doubted my abilities– I just used everything I had.

  Having confidence in our own ability to cope with the stresses of life can play an important part in resilience. Becoming more confident in our own abilities, including our ability to respond to and deal with a crisis, is a great way to build resilience for the future. So, remove the doubt. You are enough. I learned I am enough.

- **Recognize negative comments in your head:** When you hear them, practice immediately replacing them with positive ones, such as, "I can do this," "I'm a great friend/mother/partner," or "I'm good at my job." Negative concepts crept into my adult head, and luckily, I have kids and a lovely bride who help me keep them out. I might also share that the idea of 'self-affirmation' is not something a lot of people (including myself) are comfortable with. Get over it… that's the point.

- **Remind yourself of your strengths and accomplishments.** This is positive affirmation work (like I just spoke about above) … And if you aren't into or comfortable with affirmation-speak, then try this instead (it's what I do): just think about your accomplishments. Remember things you have achieved. Rerun them in your head and see what made them work. Recall when your strengths served you well. Dwell on them. Give that a try– your brain will behave accordingly.

- **Staying optimistic** during dark periods can be difficult, but maintaining a hopeful outlook is an important part of resilience. What you or I may be dealing with may be difficult, but it's important to remain hopeful and positive about a brighter future. This goes back to 'seeing through it'… but it's a critical tool.

- **Positive thinking** does not mean ignoring the problem in order to focus on positive outcomes. It means understanding that setbacks are temporary and that you have the skills and abilities to combat the challenges you face. This is a key to successful living that I incorporate into my coaching work with professionals facing difficult situations and decisions. You and I can choose this as a mindset. I recommend it highly.

My very best to you… Dom

Be Brave: Resources

I regret having said a joke. I've said it out loud more than once. It's dark humor on my part. But I do have a sense of humor that is part of my Resilience toolkit. So, I suppose it shows up when I want to laugh instead of cry.

I joked about my parents' alcoholism, particularly my mom's. I said, "…that it made sense that she was an alcoholic—she had to deal with us five boys growing up."

In a dark humor kind of way, that is funny, but more important is the truth: alcoholism, drug abuse, the poor choices and hell in life they lead to, and then add suicide, broken families, incarceration, and physical abuse... well, these are all very far from funny.

My family could have benefited from these numbers at one time or another… all the way into adulthood. But we never called anyone. We weren't brave enough or aware enough. **But you are both aware and brave enough.**

If you need these numbers, know you are loved and worth the call.

Be brave:

- **988 Suicide & Crisis Lifeline**
Text: 988
Chat: https://www.mhanational.org/resources/988.

- **National Alliance on Mental Illness (NAMI)**
Helpline: 800-950-6264,
Text "helpline" to: 62640
Chat: https://www.nami.org

- **Substance Abuse and Mental Health**
Helpline: (800) 662-4357
Online: https://www.apa.org

About the author:

Dom's most valued titles: Husband, Dad, Grampa.

Dominic Wharram lives in Minnesota with his wife, Linda. Retired as a corporate executive from a Fortune 5 company and finally blooming. Dom's an empty nester (three grown children, all with growing families); he remains a servant leader working with small companies and start-ups as a strategic advisor and executive coach.

Dom is also an author of both fiction and non-fiction works and offers a unique keynote address to educator groups with a special message of gratitude loosely based on 'Resilience Now'.

*Find **Dom** in any of these places:*

Publisher: **dCoached.com**

LinkedIn: **www.linkedin.com/in/domwharram/**

Instagram (new!): **@DomWharram**

Share with others: **Resilient-Now.com**

More resources: **www.Resilient-Now.org**

www.ingramcontent.com/pod-product-compliance
Lightning Source LLC
Chambersburg PA
CBHW070448050426
42451CB00015B/3384